MW01136058

# PEOPLE'S BIBLE COMMENTARY

# PSALMS II

## JOHN F. BRUG

CONCORDIA PUBLISHING HOUSE · SAINT LOUIS

Revised edition first printed in 2005.
Copyright © 1992 Concordia Publishing House
3558 S. Jefferson Ave., St. Louis, MO 63118-3968
1-800-325-3040 · www.cph.org

All rights reserved. No part of this publication may be reproduced, stored in a retrieval system, or transmitted, in any form or by any means, electronic, mechanical, photocopying, recording, or otherwise, without the prior written permission of Concordia Publishing House.

Commentary and pictures are reprinted from PSALMS 73–150 (The People's Bible Series), copyright © 1989 by Northwestern Publishing House. Used by permission.

Interior illustrations by Glenn Myers.

Unless otherwise stated, the Scripture quotations in this publication are taken from the HOLY BIBLE, NEW INTERNATIONAL VERSION®. NIV®. Copyright © 1973, 1978, 1984 by International Bible Society. Used by permission of Zondervan Publishing House. All rights reserved.

Manufactured in the United States of America

ISBN 0-7586-0428-9

1 2 3 4 5 6 7 8 9 10    14 13 12 11 10 09 08 07 06 05

# CONTENTS

## ILLUSTRATIONS

## MAP

# EDITOR'S PREFACE

The *People's Bible Commentary* is just what the name implies—a Bible and commentary for the people. It includes the complete text of the Holy Scriptures in the popular New International Version. The commentary following the Scripture sections contains personal applications as well as historical background and explanations of the text.

The authors of the *People's Bible Commentary* are men of scholarship and practical insight gained from years of experience in the teaching and preaching ministries. They have tried to avoid the technical jargon which limits so many commentary series to professional Bible scholars.

The most important feature of these books is that they are Christ-centered. Speaking of the Old Testament Scriptures, Jesus himself declared, "These are the Scriptures that testify about me" (John 5:39). Each volume of the *People's Bible Commentary* directs our attention to Jesus Christ. He is the center of the entire Bible. He is our only Savior.

We dedicate these volumes to the glory of God and to the good of his people.

The Publishers

# INTRODUCTION TO PSALMS 73–150

This volume is a continuation of The People's Bible commentary on the book of Psalms. Consult *Psalms I* for a general introduction to the book of Psalms and for the commentary on Psalms 1 to 72.

# BOOK THREE

## *Psalms 73–89*

The book of Psalms consists of five subdivisions called books. The third "book" of Psalms is made up of Psalms 73 to 89. These psalms are grouped together primarily on the basis of authorship. Book 3 can be divided into two main groups.

Psalms 73 to 83 are attributed to Asaph, a temple musician from the time of David. These psalms are concerned mainly with the history and welfare of Mount Zion, the mountain on which the temple was built. These psalms prefer the divine name God.

Psalms 84 to 89 are all attributed to the sons of Korah, except for Psalm 86, which is by David. Psalms 88 and 89 each have a second heading that attributes them to Heman the Ezrahite and Ethan the Ezrahite, respectively. Heman and Ethan were apparently members of the sons of Korah. The sons of Korah were a group of temple musicians who were descended from Korah, the leader of a rebellion against Moses and Aaron during the years of wandering in the wilderness of Sinai. Like the psalms of Asaph, this collection of psalms is concerned with the welfare of the people of Israel and the temple. These psalms prefer the divine name Lord.

# Psalm 73

## *Why do the wicked prosper?*

Psalm 73 serves as an excellent introduction to Book 3 of Psalms, which ponders the problem of the suffering of God's people Israel at the hands of their enemies. How could it be fair for ungodly heathen nations like Assyria and Babylon to enjoy prosperity and power while God's chosen people Israel suffered defeat and captivity? How could a just, powerful God allow such things to happen? This is the main problem addressed in Book 3 of Psalms.

Although Psalm 73 makes an excellent introduction to a consideration of the historical problem Israel faced, it has a much wider application. Since the psalm speaks in very general terms, it is applicable to every problem that troubles believers of every time and place. Today too believers are angered when they see drug dealers and pornographers getting rich. They are troubled when they hear of oppressive dictators stashing away fortunes in Swiss bank accounts. How can a just God allow such injustice? Psalm 73 answers this perennial question.

### *The problem*

**A psalm of Asaph.**

¹ **Surely God is good to Israel,**
**to those who are pure in heart.**

² **But as for me, my feet had almost slipped;**
**I had nearly lost my foothold.**
³ **For I envied the arrogant**
**when I saw the prosperity of the wicked.**

Asaph knew and believed that God is good to his people and that he punishes the wicked. But Asaph's observations of the real world seemed to contradict what he believed. When he looked around, he saw many godly people suffering. He saw many wicked people prospering. Perhaps his belief had been wrong. He thought: "Maybe God really does not care about right and wrong. Maybe God is powerless to destroy evil. Maybe there is no God."

The prosperity of the wicked was so troubling to Asaph that he was in danger of losing his faith. He therefore decided to think more about this problem.

## *The prosperity of the wicked*

⁴They have no struggles;
their bodies are healthy and strong.
⁵They are free from the burdens common to man;
they are not plagued by human ills.

⁶Therefore pride is their necklace;
they clothe themselves with violence.
⁷From their callous hearts comes iniquity;
the evil conceits of their minds know no limits.
⁸They scoff, and speak with malice;
in their arrogance they threaten oppression.
⁹Their mouths lay claim to heaven,
and their tongues take possession of the earth.

¹⁰Therefore their people turn to them
and drink up waters in abundance.
¹¹They say, "How can God know?
Does the Most High have knowledge?"
¹²This is what the wicked are like—
always carefree, they increase in wealth.

At first Asaph's meditation did him no good. It simply strengthened his doubts. Not only were the wicked rich and powerful; it seemed that their wickedness was the chief cause of their riches and power. It seemed that crime did pay. To make matters worse, these evildoers were proud of their wickedness. They boasted about their sins like the present-day sinners who go on talk shows to revel in their sins or who write books to gain wealth from their wickedness. Like present-day scoffers, they spoke arrogant words against God.

Verse 10, "Therefore their people turn to them and drink up waters in abundance," is difficult to translate and to explain. It appears to mean that some weak-willed people are so impressed by the prosperity of the wicked that they join up with them in order to share in their ill-gotten gains. They say: "It's obvious that God either does not know or does not care about the evil deeds of the powerful, so we might as well follow their example. Then we will be as rich and powerful as they are." This kind of thinking sounded so plausible that it was starting to sound good even to Asaph.

## The turning point

[13] **Surely in vain have I kept my heart pure;**
**in vain have I washed my hands in innocence.**
[14] **All day long I have been plagued;**
**I have been punished every morning.**

[15] **If I had said, "I will speak thus,"**
**I would have betrayed your children.**
[16] **When I tried to understand all this,**
**it was oppressive to me**
[17] **till I entered the sanctuary of God;**
**then I understood their final destiny.**

Asaph was on the brink of a terrible fall. This thought flickered through his mind: "Surely in vain have I kept my heart pure; in vain have I washed my hands in innocence" (verse 13). It seemed like a waste of time to be a believer. But that very thought shocked Asaph back to reality. Why was he serving God? Was it just to get something for himself, or was it because he loved God? Why was he doing good? Was it to earn something for himself, or was it because it was the right thing to do? On the brink of disaster, Asaph woke up and began to think more clearly. He realized that he had to look beyond present appearances to ultimate, eternal realities.

## The solution

> $^{18}$Surely you place them on slippery ground;
>   you cast them down to ruin.
> $^{19}$How suddenly are they destroyed,
>   completely swept away by terrors!
> $^{20}$As a dream when one awakes, so when you arise,
>   O Lord, you will despise them as fantasies.
>
> $^{21}$When my heart was grieved and my spirit embittered,
> $^{22}$I was senseless and ignorant;
>   I was a brute beast before you.
>
> $^{23}$Yet I am always with you;
>   you hold me by my right hand.
> $^{24}$You guide me with your counsel,
>   and afterward you will take me into glory.
> $^{25}$Whom have I in heaven but you?
>   And earth has nothing I desire besides you.
> $^{26}$My flesh and my heart may fail,
>   but God is the strength of my heart
>   and my portion forever.

<sup>27</sup> Those who are far from you will perish;
you destroy all who are unfaithful to you.

<sup>28</sup> But as for me, it is good to be near God.
I have made the Sovereign LORD my refuge;
I will tell of all your deeds.

Asaph realized that the problem which was perplexing him was resolved by two unshakable facts.

One was the certain judgment of the wicked. Though they are in a lofty position now, they are perched on a slippery slope. They can and will be swept away in a moment. Their fall may occur in this lifetime. Fortunes can be lost in a day. Respected leaders fall into disgrace and disfavor. Gangsters are "rubbed out," and dictators are overthrown or assassinated. Yes, the wicked do indeed stand on slippery ground.

But even if they manage to hang on to their wealth and power until the end of their lives, they cannot take anything with them. Like the rich man who ignored poor Lazarus, they will find themselves in hell, where their former wealth and power will do them no good. They will endure an eternal death, separated from the grace of God and all his blessings. What will it profit such a man to have gained the whole world if he loses his own soul?

Asaph wondered how he could have been so stupid as to almost fall for the deceptive lures of the ungodly. Not only are the ill-gotten gains of the ungodly sure to be snatched away from them, but Asaph already had something far better than their riches and fame—the favor and the presence of God. Asaph remembered that the greatest riches of the believer are not the earthly or eternal blessings God gives us, wonderful as those are. Believers' greatest treasure is God himself. Fellowship with God is theirs, now and forever. They always have this blessing, even though the situation on earth may look bleak for the moment.

Comforted by this truth, Asaph finds strength to look beyond the problems of the present to the fellowship he enjoys with God now and to the even more glorious form this fellowship will assume in eternity. With his faith renewed, Asaph expresses his delight in his relationship with God. The psalm closes triumphantly with a confession of Asaph's faith and his promise to share the good news of God's great deeds with others.

The story of Asaph's victory over doubt is a valuable lesson for us, because we often struggle with the same doubts. When we are disturbed or angered by the seeming prosperity of the wicked, like Asaph we should look beyond present appearances to the ultimate outcome. Then, like Asaph, we can overcome our doubts and wait patiently for the just judgment of God, who will punish every evil and reward all those who have remained faithful to him.

# Psalm 74

## *The destruction of the temple*

Psalm 74 is an appropriate follow-up to Psalm 73, since it elaborates on a specific example of the triumph of the ungodly, namely, the destruction of the temple in Jerusalem by the Babylonians. Psalm 74 is closely related to Psalms 78 and 79, which also speak of the destruction of Jerusalem. Another common denominator of these three psalms and several other psalms of Asaph is their emphasis on God as the shepherd of Israel.

The heading of this psalm reads, "A *maskil* of Asaph." The meaning of *maskil* is uncertain, but it appears to mean either a "skillful psalm" or an "instructive psalm." The musician Asaph was a contemporary of King David. The destruction of the temple described in Psalm 74 occurred in 586 B.C., about four hundred years after the life of Asaph.

This has led some commentators to suggest that this psalm was not written by the Asaph of David's day but by a later descendant of Asaph, perhaps one who shared his name. According to this theory, the term "Asaph" would refer not only to one individual but to a succession of musicians from one family.

However, this psalm could have been written by the Asaph of David's time through prophetic inspiration, just as Moses in Deuteronomy chapter 28 wrote of the fall of Jerusalem long before it happened.

Asaph may have written Psalm 74 at a time when Israel was carried away with enthusiasm because of the construction of the temple. His purpose may have been to look ahead to the ultimate fate of the temple. Just as Moses' prophecy sounded a solemn warning on the eve of the entry into the Promised Land, Asaph sounded a similar warning on the eve of the construction of the temple. His testimony, like that of Moses, would serve as a warning throughout the history of Israel.

It would also serve as a comfort at the time when the prophecy was fulfilled, since the foretelling of the destruction would show that even this terrible catastrophe was not outside of God's plan and control. This psalm could then serve as a prayer for relief from this disaster.

11

## *Introductory plea*

**A *maskil* of Asaph.**

¹**Why have you rejected us forever, O God?**
**Why does your anger smolder**
**against the sheep of your pasture?**

²**Remember the people you purchased of old,**
**the tribe of your inheritance, whom you redeemed—**
**Mount Zion, where you dwelt.**
³**Turn your steps toward these everlasting ruins,**
**all this destruction the enemy has brought**
**on the sanctuary.**

To the faithful in Israel, the destruction of the temple, which served as a symbol of God's presence, was evidence that God had deserted them. But this seemed inconsistent with the love God had shown them when he had adopted them as his chosen people, when he had given them the Promised Land, and when his glory had appeared in Solomon's temple. Surely he would not leave his people in this condition.

## *The destruction*

⁴**Your foes roared in the place**
**where you met with us;**
**they set up their standards as signs.**
⁵**They behaved like men wielding axes**
**to cut through a thicket of trees.**
⁶**They smashed all the carved paneling**
**with their axes and hatchets.**
⁷**They burned your sanctuary to the ground;**
**they defiled the dwelling place of your Name.**
⁸**They said in their hearts,**
**"We will crush them completely!"**
**They burned every place**
**where God was worshiped in the land.**

When the Babylonians destroyed Jerusalem and the temple, the devastation was complete. Many years later, when Nehemiah came to rebuild the walls of the city, the piles of rubble were still so large that they hindered his tour around the city.

The reference in verse 8 to the destruction of "every place where God was worshiped in the land" is puzzling, since there was only one legitimate temple in Israel. It could refer to local nonsacrificial places of worship like synagogues, but there is no evidence that local synagogues existed before the exile.

It is unlikely that Asaph would lament the destruction of illegitimate high places, which were scattered throughout the land, but he may be referring simply to all the cities throughout Israel from which true worshipers came to Jerusalem. Perhaps the reference is to the destruction of the temple and to the much earlier destruction of the tabernacle at Shiloh. Though separate in time, these two events were parallel in significance and impact, as we will see in later psalms of Asaph.

The destruction of Jerusalem gave the Babylonians pride both in their might and in the superiority of their gods. This pride and the cruelty that accompanied it called for a response from God, but no such answer seemed to be forthcoming.

## The desertion

> ⁹We are given no miraculous signs;
>  no prophets are left,
>  and none of us knows how long this will be.
> ¹⁰How long will the enemy mock you, O God?
>  Will the foe revile your name forever?
> ¹¹Why do you hold back your hand, your right hand?
>  Take it from the folds of your garment
>            and destroy them!

13

After the destruction of Jerusalem, it seemed that God had deserted the remnant that remained in the land. The prophets Ezekiel and Daniel were with the exiles in Babylon. Jeremiah had remained in Judah, but the majority of the survivors rejected his leadership, and he was forcibly taken to Egypt. In the midst of these circumstances, which are described in Jeremiah chapters 41 to 44, the situation seemed hopeless, but the faithful few would not give up hope.

*God's past goodness*

> [12] **But you, O God, are my king from of old;**
> **you bring salvation upon the earth.**
> [13] **It was you who split open the sea by your power;**
> **you broke the heads of the monster in the waters.**
> [14] **It was you who crushed the heads of Leviathan**
> **and gave him as food to the creatures**
> **of the desert.**
> [15] **It was you who opened up springs and streams;**
> **you dried up the ever flowing rivers.**
> [16] **The day is yours, and yours also the night;**
> **you established the sun and moon.**
> [17] **It was you who set all the boundaries**
> **of the earth;**
> **you made both summer and winter.**

To some in Israel, it might have seemed that God did nothing because he could do nothing. But such a notion was disproved by the power God had shown in creation. Though these verses refer primarily to creation, they also reminded the listeners of the exodus from Egypt. In Israel's poetic language, both the waters of the sea that God "tamed" on the third day of creation and the nation of Egypt dwelling along the mighty Nile River were sometimes pictured as a sea monster. Leviathan was one name for this monster. By using this term, Asaph creates a double reference that reminds the people of God's creative as well as his redemptive power. This power was their hope.

## *Plea for relief*

> [18] **Remember how the enemy has mocked you, O Lord,**
> **how foolish people have reviled your name.**
> [19] **Do not hand over the life of your dove**
> **to wild beasts;**
> **do not forget the lives of your afflicted people forever.**
> [20] **Have regard for your covenant,**
> **because haunts of violence fill**
> **the dark places of the land.**
> [21] **Do not let the oppressed retreat in disgrace;**
> **may the poor and needy praise your name.**
> [22] **Rise up, O God, and defend your cause;**
> **remember how fools mock you all day long.**
> [23] **Do not ignore the clamor of your adversaries,**
> **the uproar of your enemies,**
> **which rises continually.**

In his closing plea, Asaph rests his case on two foundations: God's honor and God's love for his people. He prays as we do in the Lord's Prayer, "Hallowed be your name." He prays for deliverance not only that he may benefit, but also that God's honor may be upheld. This will be done when the arrogant boasts of the Babylonians about the power of their gods are silenced.

By using the affectionate lovers' name "dove" as God's name for his beloved bride, Asaph stresses the greatness of God's love for Israel. He appeals to the covenant promises that God had made to Israel as his bride and begs him to restore their union. Psalm 74 closes with a note of hope, but the full answer to this plea will be forthcoming only in the psalms that follow.

# Psalm 75

## *The God of history*

Psalm 75 answers this question raised by Psalm 74: "How long will the enemy mock?" They will continue in their arrogance only until God, who raised them up to be the instruments of his judgment against Israel, brings judgment upon them in their turn.

We see how this psalm was fulfilled in history: God raised up Assyria to crush the idolatrous northern kingdom of Israel and to chastise the wayward kingdom of Judah. But when the time was right, he raised up Babylon to destroy both arrogant Assyria and unrepentant Judah. After the 70 years of Judah's captivity in Babylon were fulfilled, God raised up Cyrus of Persia to destroy Babylon and to restore his people to their land. God rules the nations and controls their history in such a way that his purposes of judgment and of blessing are fulfilled. For this we thank and praise him.

For the director of music. ⸤To the tune of⸥ "Do Not Destroy."
A psalm of Asaph. A song.

¹We give thanks to you, O God,
  we give thanks, for your Name is near;
  men tell of your wonderful deeds.

² You say, "I choose the appointed time;
  it is I who judge uprightly.
³When the earth and all its people quake,
    it is I who hold its pillars firm.                    *Selah*

⁴To the arrogant I say, 'Boast no more,'
  and to the wicked, 'Do not lift up your horns.

⁵ Do not lift your horns against heaven;
  do not speak with outstretched neck.'"

⁶ No one from the east or the west
  or from the desert can exalt a man.
⁷ But it is God who judges:
  He brings one down, he exalts another.
⁸ In the hand of the LORD is a cup
      full of foaming wine mixed with spices;
  he pours it out,
  and all the wicked of the earth drink it
      down to its very dregs.

⁹ As for me, I will declare this forever;
  I will sing praise to the God of Jacob.
¹⁰ I will cut off the horns of all the wicked,
  but the horns of the righteous will be lifted up.

This psalm is a proclamation of God's rule over history. This rule provides a theme for the hymns of God's people throughout time and into eternity. The people of Israel sang of victory on the shores of the Red Sea (Exodus 15). Hannah, Mary, and Zechariah all rejoiced in the Lord's triumph over the enemies of his people (1 Samuel 2; Luke 1). Saints and angels in heaven will echo their song (Revelation 15,19).

Believers recognize that God controls both the script and the schedule of history. Often his hand is invisible except to the eyes of faith. We see only the human actors and their motives. At times it seems that society is falling to pieces and civilization is collapsing. But God in his providence overrules the plans and intentions of the world rulers. He turns the course of events so that his people are preserved and his promises are fulfilled.

This psalm uses two figures of speech that are very common in Scripture. Horns are a symbol of power. The horns of the wicked will be cut off; the horns of the righteous, lifted up. The world rulers will be stripped of their power, but God's people will exercise power with him throughout eternity. A cup of wine is frequently used as a symbol of God's judgment because the folly and confusion of those who oppose God is like the folly and confusion of those intoxicated with wine.

Psalm 75 begins and ends with praise. To join in the praise of this psalm, we must first know the deeds God has performed in history. When we understand these deeds, the meaning of God's saving name will be near and dear to us. We study God's deeds so that we will be moved to praise him. We proclaim God's deeds so that others will be moved to join our praises.

# Psalm 76

## *The God of victory*

Like Psalm 75, Psalm 76 answers the question and complaint voiced in Psalm 74. Psalm 75 states the general principle that God rules over kings and world rulers. Psalm 76 goes one step further and describes an example of such a victory. Although the psalm names no specific occasion, the circumstances described in the psalm fit the situation at the time of the destruction of the army of the Assyrian King Sennacherib in 701 B.C. (Isaiah 36,37). If this psalm was in fact written in response to that occasion, it raises the same question of authorship that was discussed in the introduction to Psalm 74.

For the director of music. With stringed instruments.
A psalm of Asaph. A song.

## *God's fame*

¹In Judah God is known;
  his name is great in Israel.
²His tent is in Salem,
  his dwelling place in Zion.

## *God's victory*

³There he broke the flashing arrows,
  the shields and the swords, the weapons of war.

                                                        **Selah**

⁴You are resplendent with light,
  more majestic than mountains rich with game.

⁵Valiant men lie plundered,
  they sleep their last sleep;
  not one of the warriors can lift his hands.
⁶At your rebuke, O God of Jacob,
  both horse and chariot lie still.

⁷You alone are to be feared.
  Who can stand before you when you are angry?
⁸From heaven you pronounced judgment,
  and the land feared and was quiet—
⁹when you, O God, rose up to judge,
  to save all the afflicted of the land.

                                                        **Selah**

## *God's fame*

¹⁰Surely your wrath against men brings you praise,
  and the survivors of your wrath are restrained.

¹¹ **Make vows to the LORD your God and fulfill them;**
**let all the neighboring lands bring gifts**
**to the One to be feared.**

¹² **He breaks the spirit of rulers;**
**he is feared by the kings of the earth.**

The psalm begins and ends with a proclamation of the fame God receives because of his victory. The opening proclamation stresses the acknowledgment he receives from his own people. Judah and Israel are the names of the two kingdoms into which the people had been divided after the time of Solomon. Salem and Zion are two names for Jerusalem, the location of the temple.

The closing proclamation turns to the recognition God receives from those who had formerly been rebelling against him. Examples from history would include those Egyptians who were awed by the plagues and took measures to deliver themselves, Rahab and the Gibeonites who joined God's people in order to escape the destruction that was coming upon the rest of the Canaanites, and the army officer who pleaded with Elijah for his life after he had witnessed the destruction of two other contingents of the army that had tried to arrest the prophet.

The general sense of verse 10 is clear, but the exact translation is difficult. Literally translated, the Hebrew says, "Wrath of man—your praise; remainder of wrath you bind." The NIV offers two translations. The rendering of the main text, "Surely your wrath against men brings you praise, and the survivors of your wrath are restrained," stresses the results of God's wrath against the ungodly. His judgments result in thanks from his own people for their deliverance. The ungodly too will "praise" him—either with the praise of repentance or with the praise of submission.

Even the vanquished in hell will bow the knee and confess that Jesus is Lord to the glory of God the Father (Philippians 2:10,11). At Christ's return even Caiaphas and his cronies will confess, "Blessed is he who comes in the name of the Lord" (Luke 13:35).

The alternate reading in the NIV footnote, "Surely the wrath of men brings you praise, and with the remainder of wrath you arm yourself," stresses the result of man's wrath against God. This translation approaches the subject from a different direction but ends up in the same place. God's wrath against men leads to God's glory, but so does man's wrath against God. This happens when man's wrath against God backfires against the rebels, and their defeat produces blessing for God's people and honor for God. The greatest example of this occurred when the hatred that Satan and the world had for Christ led them to crucify him, but his death produced their greatest defeat and the triumph of God's plan of salvation.

The middle verses of the psalm describe the victory of God over his enemies. Verses 3 to 6 seem to be a description of a historical event that took place at the city of Jerusalem, most likely the destruction of the Assyrian army by the angel of death. However, like Psalm 46, this psalm seems to reach beyond the history of the earthly Jerusalem to the history of God's spiritual Jerusalem, the church. In both the Old and New Testaments, the final victory of God's people against the attacks of Satan and the world is described as the rescue of Jerusalem from its enemies (Ezekiel 38,39; Revelation 20). God's great victories in Old Testament history point to his final victory on the Last Day, when the complaint of Psalm 74 will be answered in full and the deliverance of God's people will be complete.

# Psalm 77

## *Will the Lord reject forever?*

Psalm 77 repeats the message of the three preceding psalms. It reviews both the question and the answer raised by the triumph of the enemies of God's people.

**For the director of music. For Jeduthun. Of Asaph. A psalm.**

Jeduthun was a temple musician contemporary with David and Asaph. If this heading is translated "for Jeduthun," it strengthens the argument that at least this Asaph psalm was written by the Asaph of David's day, not by some later namesake or descendant. However, the Hebrew expression here is not the same as the one in the heading of Psalm 39, which should be translated "to or for Jeduthun." This heading, like the heading of Psalm 62, may be translated "according to Jeduthun." This translation would suggest that the psalm was to be played according to Jeduthun's tune or style of music. In this case, the heading would be less decisive evidence for tying the psalm to David's time.

## *The question*

<sup>1</sup>I cried out to God for help;
I cried out to God to hear me.
<sup>2</sup>When I was in distress, I sought the Lord;
at night I stretched out untiring hands
and my soul refused to be comforted.
<sup>3</sup>I remembered you, O God, and I groaned;
I mused, and my spirit grew faint.                    *Selah*
<sup>4</sup>You kept my eyes from closing;
I was too troubled to speak.
<sup>5</sup>I thought about the former days,
        the years of long ago;

⁶I remembered my songs in the night.
My heart mused and my spirit inquired:
⁷ "Will the Lord reject forever?
Will he never show his favor again?
⁸ Has his unfailing love vanished forever?
Has his promise failed for all time?
⁹ Has God forgotten to be merciful?
Has he in anger withheld his compassion?"

*Selah*

This opening plea has the same intense, personal tone as Psalm 73. The psalmist is deeply shaken and suffers great spiritual anguish because of the catastrophe that has befallen Israel and Judah. He can understand that God would chasten and correct his wayward people, but this disaster is so complete and seems so inescapable that it appears the Lord has forsaken his people and abandoned his covenant with them. The psalmist is distressed when he contrasts the present suffering of the Israelites with their past blessings, but it is in this very recollection of past history that Asaph begins to find the solution to his problem.

## The answer

¹⁰Then I thought,
"To this I will appeal:
the years of the right hand of the Most High."
¹¹I will remember the deeds of the LORD;
yes, I will remember your miracles of long ago.
¹²I will meditate on all your works
and consider all your mighty deeds.

¹³ Your ways, O God, are holy.
What god is so great as our God?
¹⁴You are the God who performs miracles;
you display your power among the peoples.

23

<sup>15</sup>**With your mighty arm you redeemed your people,**
**the descendants of Jacob and Joseph.**

***Selah***

<sup>16</sup> **The waters saw you,**
**O God, the waters saw you and writhed;**
**the very depths were convulsed.**
<sup>17</sup> **The clouds poured down water,**
**the skies resounded with thunder;**
**your arrows flashed back and forth.**
<sup>18</sup> **Your thunder was heard in the whirlwind,**
**your lightning lit up the world;**
**the earth trembled and quaked.**
<sup>19</sup> **Your path led through the sea,**
**your way through the mighty waters,**
**though your footprints were not seen.**

<sup>20</sup> **You led your people like a flock**
**by the hand of Moses and Aaron.**

In Psalm 73 the author looked to the future for comfort. In Psalm 74 and here, he looks to the past. The language that refers to victory over the sea is similar to that of Psalm 74, but in that psalm the emphasis was on God's creative power, which ruled over the sea at creation. Here the emphasis shifts to God's redeeming power, which controlled the sea during the exodus from Egypt. "The years of the right hand of the Most High" (verse 10) are the years in which God used his almighty power to deliver his people from Egypt and lead them into their own land.

The mighty acts of God against the Egyptians were holy and just, because the Egyptians had oppressed Israel and despised the warnings God had given through Moses. In the same way, the Canaanites brought judgment upon themselves by their immoral idolatry.

The waters are divided

The crossing of the sea is described in very picturesque language. The account in Exodus chapter 14 mentions a strong wind and the cloud that terrified the Egyptians, but it says nothing about rain, thunder, and lightning at the crossing of the Red Sea, so some of the language of this psalm may be figurative. However, the psalm may simply be adding details about the storm that were not mentioned in Exodus.

The psalm closes on a note of comfort with the "Good Shepherd" theme, which is typical of this group of psalms. In times of trouble, the Israelites looked to the past and remembered how God their shepherd had led them out of Egypt. In times of trouble, we remember how the Good Shepherd gave his life for the sheep. Since Christ loved us and gave himself to redeem us from our sins, no trial or disaster can separate us from his love. As God led his flock to the Promised Land by the hand of Moses and Aaron, so he is now leading his flock to their eternal home by the hand of Christ, the Good Shepherd.

# Psalm 78

### *How often they rebelled*

Psalm 78 considers Israel's suffering from another angle. It was true that Israel's enemies were wicked people whose triumph was perplexing, but the majority of the people of Israel could hardly claim to be innocent victims. They had provoked God and brought disaster upon themselves by their persistent disobedience and idolatry.

Psalm 78 was apparently written to celebrate the establishment of David's dynasty in Jerusalem because this event led to the building of the temple. Later in Israel's history, this psalm would serve a double purpose. During the years of idolatry and rebellion in the divided kingdom, it would stand as a warning against repeating the folly of the wilderness years and the time of the judges. Then during the captivity, it would offer a ray of hope by reminding the Israelites that one of the brightest moments of their past had arisen out of the depths of disaster and that history could repeat itself.

The poetic structure of this psalm is complex, with many departures from strict parallelism and with many long run-on lines. (A few of the following lines are divided on the basis of English length rather than Hebrew accents.)

## A solemn call to hear

**A *maskil* of Asaph.**

¹**O my people, hear my teaching;**
**listen to the words of my mouth.**
²**I will open my mouth in parables,**
**I will utter hidden things, things from of old—**
    ³ **what we have heard and known,**
    **what our fathers have told us.**
⁴**We will not hide them from their children;**
**we will tell the next generation**
        **the praiseworthy deeds of the LORD,**
        **his power, and the wonders he has done.**

⁵ **He decreed statutes for Jacob**
**and established the law in Israel,**
**which he commanded our forefathers**
        **to teach their children,**
⁶**so the next generation would know them,**
**even the children yet to be born,**
**and they in turn would tell their children.**
⁷**Then they would put their trust in God**
**and would not forget his deeds**
**but would keep his commands.**

**⁸They would not be like their forefathers—
a stubborn and rebellious generation,
whose hearts were not loyal to God,
whose spirits were not faithful to him.**

This introduction stresses the depth and the permanent relevance of God's revelation to Israel. The depth of the revelation is stressed by the words "parables" and "hidden things" (verse 2). The teachings of this psalm are "hidden" because they can be known and understood only through the revelation of the Holy Spirit. The word translated "parables" refers to any kind of message that requires careful study and comparison with the listeners' own situations before they can understand it properly and apply it correctly. Such messages may be expressed in figurative language, like Solomon's proverbs or Jesus' parables, or they may take the form of a review of past history, as in this psalm or Stephen's sermon in Acts chapter 7.

In either case the listeners must think carefully about the meaning of the saying and apply the truth it expresses to their own situations. In Matthew 13:35 this verse is quoted in connection with Jesus' parables. This is appropriate, since all of Jesus' teaching, whether figurative or literal, served exactly the same purpose as this psalm—it warned Israel against the folly of repeating the sins of its ancestors.

The permanent and enduring relevance of God's Word is shown by the emphasis on passing it from one generation to another. The book of Deuteronomy stresses the importance of transmitting the experience of the exodus and conquest to the coming generations. This message is so prominent in Deuteronomy that the words "Do Not Forget" could be used as the theme of that book. This psalm echoes the tone of a chapter such as Deuteronomy chapter 6.

The practical importance of such teaching is shown by the warning that the children can escape judgment only if they learn from the sad experience of their ancestors and do not repeat their sin. In 1 Corinthians chapter 10, Paul tells us that the stories of the exodus serve the same purpose for us as they did for Israel: "If you think you are standing firm, be careful that you don't fall!" (verse 12).

## The rebellion

> <sup>9</sup>**The men of Ephraim, though armed with bows,**
> **turned back on the day of battle;**
> <sup>10</sup>**they did not keep God's covenant**
> **and refused to live by his law.**
> <sup>11</sup>**They forgot what he had done,**
> **the wonders he had shown them.**

It is difficult to see any reason why the tribe of Ephraim would be singled out for criticism concerning their behavior during the exodus or conquest. They did not take a lead in the rebellions of the wilderness years. They did not have a reputation for cowardice in battle. They are probably singled out because of their later leadership in the secession of the northern kingdom of Israel under Jeroboam. This reference probably intends to compare their secession with the rebellion led by Korah during the wilderness years and to place their idolatry into the same category as that of the wilderness years. The comparison is apt because in both cases we see the same rejection of God's chosen leaders and the same worship of calf gods as the representation of the Lord.

The following sections of the psalm contrast the repeated rebellion of Israel with the enduring grace of God. As you read, note the contrasts indicated by words like "but" and "yet."

## God's goodness in the wilderness

¹²He did miracles in the sight of their fathers
  in the land of Egypt, in the region of Zoan.
¹³He divided the sea and led them through;
  he made the water stand firm like a wall.
¹⁴He guided them with the cloud by day
  and with light from the fire all night.
¹⁵He split the rocks in the desert
  and gave them water as abundant as the seas;
¹⁶he brought streams out of a rocky crag
  and made water flow down like rivers.

## Israel's rebellion in the wilderness

¹⁷But they continued to sin against him,
  rebelling in the desert against the Most High.
¹⁸They willfully put God to the test
      by demanding the food they craved.

¹⁹They spoke against God, saying,
      "Can God spread a table in the desert?
    ²⁰When he struck the rock, water gushed out,
    and streams flowed abundantly.
    But can he also give us food?
    Can he supply meat for his people?"

## God's judgment in the wilderness

²¹When the Lord heard them, he was very angry;
  his fire broke out against Jacob,
  and his wrath rose against Israel,
    ²²for they did not believe in God
    or trust in his deliverance.

## God's mercy in the wilderness

²³Yet he gave a command to the skies above
  and opened the doors of the heavens;

²⁴he rained down manna for the people to eat,
  he gave them the grain of heaven.
²⁵Men ate the bread of angels;
  he sent them all the food they could eat.
²⁶He let loose the east wind from the heavens
  and led forth the south wind by his power.
²⁷He rained meat down on them like dust,
  flying birds like sand on the seashore.
²⁸He made them come down inside their camp,
      all around their tents.
²⁹They ate till they had more than enough,
  for he had given them what they craved.

## The cycle continues

³⁰But before they turned from the food they craved,
  even while it was still in their mouths,
³¹God's anger rose against them;
  he put to death the sturdiest among them,
  cutting down the young men of Israel.

³²In spite of all this, they kept on sinning;
  in spite of his wonders, they did not believe.
³³So he ended their days in futility
  and their years in terror.

³⁴Whenever God slew them, they would seek him;
  they eagerly turned to him again.
³⁵They remembered that God was their Rock,
  that God Most High was their Redeemer.

³⁶But then they would flatter him with their mouths,
  lying to him with their tongues;
³⁷their hearts were not loyal to him,
  they were not faithful to his covenant.

<sup>38</sup> Yet he was merciful;
he forgave their iniquities
and did not destroy them.
Time after time he restrained his anger
and did not stir up his full wrath.
<sup>39</sup> He remembered that they were but flesh,
a passing breeze that does not return.

<sup>40</sup> How often they rebelled against him in the desert
and grieved him in the wasteland!
<sup>41</sup> Again and again they put God to the test;
they vexed the Holy One of Israel.

The psalm intertwines two themes. The goodness of God in leading Israel from Zoan (their dwelling place in Egypt) to Zion (the permanent home of the temple) is contrasted with Israel's persistent ingratitude. There is much repetition in this psalm because already during the wilderness years there was much repetition of the same sins. For an illustration of this compare Exodus chapters 15 to 17 with Numbers chapters 11, 16, and 20.

How quickly the Israelites forgot God's power in Egypt and his promise of the land ahead of them! Therefore God did indeed send severe chastening judgments during the wilderness years, but he also continued to provide the ungrateful people with the food they needed, just as he today still provides food for the good and the evil, for the thankful and the forgetful.

The manna, wonderful as it was, could be called "bread from heaven" only in a limited sense. It appeared without human labor or effort and could prolong earthly life, but it could do no more. The manna tested Israel's faith and trust in God, but a more urgent test was coming. That test concerned the true bread from heaven. John chapter 6 tells us how Jesus fed five thousand men with a few loaves. Those who saw the miracle were briefly excited about the bread, but they wanted no part of the true Bread of Life. Their reaction to God's gift was like that of Israel in the wilderness.

In the wilderness the people of Israel did sometimes show repentance, but it was usually superficial and short-lived. Like the dew on the grass, it vanished in the heat of the sun. The sad story was repeated again and again during the wilderness years. Their unbelief was especially shocking because God had so fully proved his power in Egypt.

## God's power displayed in Egypt (Exodus 5–14)

> <sup>42</sup>They did not remember his power—
>   the day he redeemed them from the oppressor,
> <sup>43</sup>the day he displayed his miraculous signs
>         in Egypt,
>   his wonders in the region of Zoan.
> <sup>44</sup>He turned their rivers to blood;
>   they could not drink from their streams.
> <sup>45</sup>He sent swarms of flies that devoured them,
>   and frogs that devastated them.
> <sup>46</sup>He gave their crops to the grasshopper,
>   their produce to the locust.
> <sup>47</sup>He destroyed their vines with hail
>   and their sycamore-figs with sleet.
> <sup>48</sup>He gave over their cattle to the hail,
>   their livestock to bolts of lightning.
> <sup>49</sup>He unleashed against them his hot anger,
>   his wrath, indignation and hostility—
>         a band of destroying angels.
> <sup>50</sup>He prepared a path for his anger;
>   he did not spare them from death
>   but gave them over to the plague.
> <sup>51</sup>He struck down all the firstborn of Egypt,
>   the firstfruits of manhood in the tents of Ham.

<sup>52</sup> But he brought his people out like a flock;
   he led them like sheep through the desert.
<sup>53</sup> He guided them safely, so they were unafraid;
   but the sea engulfed their enemies.


## *God's power displayed in Canaan (Joshua)*

<sup>54</sup> Thus he brought them to the border
         of his holy land,
   to the hill country his right hand had taken.
<sup>55</sup> He drove out nations before them
   and allotted their lands to them
   as an inheritance;
   he settled the tribes of Israel in their homes.

We might think that once Israel was established in its own land, the rebellion of the wilderness years would come to an end. But instead of thanking God for the bounty of their land, the Israelites gave credit to the idols of the land and served them in the place of the Lord.


## *Rebellion in the land (Judges)*

<sup>56</sup> But they put God to the test
   and rebelled against the Most High;
   they did not keep his statutes.
<sup>57</sup> Like their fathers they were disloyal
         and faithless,
   as unreliable as a faulty bow.
<sup>58</sup> They angered him with their high places;
   they aroused his jealousy with their idols.


## *Judgment in the land*

<sup>59</sup> When God heard them, he was very angry;
   he rejected Israel completely.

34

⁶⁰He abandoned the tabernacle of Shiloh,
  the tent he had set up among men.
⁶¹He sent the ark of his might into captivity,
  his splendor into the hands of the enemy.
⁶²He gave his people over to the sword;
  he was very angry with his inheritance.
⁶³Fire consumed their young men,
  and their maidens had no wedding songs;
⁶⁴their priests were put to the sword,
  and their widows could not weep.

The destruction of the tabernacle at Shiloh apparently
took place when the Philistines captured the ark of the
covenant during the days of Eli (1 Samuel 4–6). It took
many years for Israel to recover from this disaster. Throughout the days of Samuel and Saul, Israel had no central sanctuary, although there was a tabernacle at Gibeon. It was
only in the days of David that the ark was brought to
Jerusalem and the preparations were made to build the temple as the one central sanctuary.

## Mercy in the land

⁶⁵Then the Lord awoke as from sleep,
  as a man wakes from the stupor of wine.
⁶⁶He beat back his enemies;
  he put them to everlasting shame.

⁶⁷Then he rejected the tents of Joseph,
  he did not choose the tribe of Ephraim;
⁶⁸but he chose the tribe of Judah,
  Mount Zion, which he loved.
⁶⁹He built his sanctuary like the heights,
  like the earth that he established forever.

⁷⁰He chose David his servant
  and took him from the sheep pens;

⁷¹ **from tending the sheep**
  **he brought him to be the shepherd**
      **of his people Jacob,**
      **of Israel his inheritance.**
⁷² **And David shepherded them with integrity of heart;**
  **with skillful hands he led them.**

God broke the power of the Philistines through the victories of David. In David he gave the people a faithful shepherd like Moses. If the Israelites had risen from the dark days of Eli to the bright days of David, they could rise again from the gloom of captivity in Babylon to the dawning of the day when the Messiah would come. He would be a shepherd far greater than Moses or David. Yet even then the sad cycle would continue. Just as many rejected Moses and David, so many would reject the Shepherd when he came. How sad that history repeats itself, but how wonderful that throughout history God's grace never fails.

# Psalm 79

## *They have reduced Jerusalem to rubble*

Psalm 79 echoes Psalm 74. The discussion of the background and authorship of that psalm applies also to this psalm.

### *The destruction and disgrace*

**A psalm of Asaph.**

¹ **O God, the nations have invaded your inheritance;**
  **they have defiled your holy temple,**
  **they have reduced Jerusalem to rubble.**
² **They have given the dead bodies of your servants**
      **as food to the birds of the air,**
  **the flesh of your saints to the beasts of the earth.**

³ They have poured out blood like water
    all around Jerusalem,
  and there is no one to bury the dead.
⁴ We are objects of reproach to our neighbors,
 of scorn and derision to those around us.

## *The prayer for justice*

⁵ How long, O LORD? Will you be angry forever?
 How long will your jealousy burn like fire?

⁶ Pour out your wrath on the nations
    that do not acknowledge you,
  on the kingdoms that do not call on your name;
    ⁷ for they have devoured Jacob
    and destroyed his homeland.

⁸ Do not hold against us the sins of the fathers;
  may your mercy come quickly to meet us,
    for we are in desperate need.

⁹ Help us, O God our Savior,
    for the glory of your name;
  deliver us and forgive our sins
    for your name's sake.

¹⁰ Why should the nations say, "Where is their God?"

  Before our eyes, make known among the nations
    that you avenge the outpoured blood of your servants.
¹¹ May the groans of the prisoners come before you;
  by the strength of your arm preserve
    those condemned to die.
¹² Pay back into the laps of our neighbors
    seven times the reproach they have hurled at you,
      O Lord.
¹³ Then we your people, the sheep of your pasture,
    will praise you forever;
  from generation to generation
    we will recount your praise.

In response to the destruction of the temple and the cruel treatment of the people of Jerusalem, the psalmist has three prayers: that God's honor be upheld, that his people be forgiven, and that his enemies be punished.

The mention of the "sins of the fathers" in verse 8 connects this psalm with Psalm 78. The faithful in Israel knew that the disaster which struck Jerusalem was due to Israel's sins, but the Babylonians thought that it was due to the weakness of Israel's god. The weak in faith among the Israelites thought that God had cast them away forever because of their sins. Both of these misunderstandings of God could be corrected with one blow if God would cast down Babylon and its allies and restore his people. Therefore the psalmist prays, "Pour out your wrath on the nations" (verse 6). When this is done, justice will be done, God's power will be demonstrated, and his love for his people will be reaffirmed.

The shepherd theme that characterizes this group of psalms brings this psalm to an end on a note of peace and comfort.

# Psalm 80

### *Hear, O Shepherd of Israel*

Psalm 80 continues the general theme of the preceding psalms, but it seems to address a different occasion. Unlike those psalms, which pointed to the destruction of Jerusalem by the Babylonians, this psalm seems to address the destruction of the northern kingdom and the near destruction of Judah by the Assyrians during the time of Hezekiah at the end of the eighth century B.C.

The mention of Ephraim and Manasseh, tribes associated with the northern kingdom, does not prove the contention of some commentators that this and other psalms which mention Joseph were written in the northern kingdom. The faithful people in Judah were always concerned about their brothers in the north. Hezekiah tried to recall the people of the north to worship in Jerusalem (2 Chronicles 30:10). Even at the time of the exile, Ezekiel prophesied the reunification of Israel (Ezekiel 37:15-28). Many of the priests and Levites in Jerusalem were exiles who left the northern kingdom to escape Jeroboam's apostasy. They naturally continued to be concerned about their former homeland. It is very likely, then, that Asaph wrote this psalm to be used as a prayer for the welfare of the people of the north, especially around the time of the destruction of Samaria in 722 B.C.

Notice the refrain that concludes major sections of the psalm. Such refrains are quite rare in the psalms.

**For the director of music. To ⌊the tune of⌋
"The Lilies of the Covenant." Of Asaph. A psalm.**

## *Opening plea*

> ¹ **Hear us, O Shepherd of Israel,**
> **you who lead Joseph like a flock;**
> **you who sit enthroned between the cherubim,**
> ² **shine forth before Ephraim, Benjamin and Manasseh.**
> **Awaken your might; come and save us.**

## *Refrain*

> ³ **Restore us, O God;**
> **make your face shine upon us,**
> **that we may be saved.**

The opening plea connects the psalm with the tribes north of Judah and speaks a prayer in their name. The following section of the psalm describes their suffering at the hands of the Assyrians, who led them into captivity.

## The problem

> ⁴O Lord **God Almighty, how long will your anger**
> **smolder against the prayers of your people?**
> ⁵**You have fed them with the bread of tears;**
> **you have made them drink tears by the bowlful.**
> ⁶**You have made us a source of contention**
> **to our neighbors,**
> **and our enemies mock us.**

## Refrain

> ⁷**Restore us, O God Almighty;**
> **make your face shine upon us,**
> **that we may be saved.**

The main body of the psalm, which follows, has three main sections. The first describes the growth of Israel under such kings as David and Solomon and the later kings Uzziah and Jeroboam II. Under such kings Israel was a prosperous, powerful kingdom that extended its influence from Egypt to the Euphrates River in the far north.

The second section describes the present desolation of the once powerful kingdom. It is like a vineyard that has had its wall broken down and is subject to destruction by wild animals. After 722 B.C. Israel never again existed as an independent kingdom, and even Judah was confined to a relatively small area of the hills of Judea.

In this psalm Israel is described as God's vine, planted in his vineyard, the Holy Land. In Scripture the vine may represent either the nation (Isaiah 5:1-7; Jeremiah 2:21) or the king of Israel (Ezekiel 17). The third section is a prayer for the king.

## Past blessing

<sup>8</sup>You brought a vine out of Egypt;
 you drove out the nations and planted it.
<sup>9</sup>You cleared the ground for it,
 and it took root and filled the land.
<sup>10</sup>The mountains were covered with its shade,
 the mighty cedars with its branches.
<sup>11</sup>It sent out its boughs to the Sea,
 its shoots as far as the River.

## Present judgment

<sup>12</sup>Why have you broken down its walls
 so that all who pass by pick its grapes?
<sup>13</sup>Boars from the forest ravage it
 and the creatures of the field feed on it.

## Prayer for the king

<sup>14</sup>Return to us, O God Almighty!
 Look down from heaven and see!
 Watch over this vine,
<sup>15</sup>the root your right hand has planted,
 the son you have raised up for yourself.
<sup>16</sup>Your vine is cut down,
 it is burned with fire;
 at your rebuke your people perish.

<sup>17</sup>Let your hand rest on the man at your right hand,
 the son of man you have raised up for yourself.

<sup>18</sup>Then we will not turn away from you;
 revive us, and we will call on your name.

## Refrain

<sup>19</sup>Restore us, O LORD God Almighty;
 make your face shine upon us,
  that we may be saved.

41

Some commentators understand the "man at [God's] right hand" (verse 17) as a figurative name for Israel, but it seems better to take it as a reference to Israel's God-given head, the king. In Israel's history it was often true, "As the king goes, so goes the nation." In the third section of the body of the psalm, the people pray for the preservation of a godly king who would stave off the disaster that was coming upon them. The northern kingdom had no such kings. All of its kings were either idolators or, worse yet, incompetent idolators.

The southern kingdom of Judah had two outstanding kings who prolonged the life of the nation, Hezekiah and Josiah. Hezekiah was king at the time of Israel's destruction and Judah's near escape from Assyria. God preserved his life for 15 extra years for the welfare of the nation. Josiah was king shortly before the destruction of Jerusalem. When he died an early death in battle, the doom of Judah was assured. The prayer of this psalm would seem to be especially fitting for Hezekiah.

However, even the best kings of Judah could not undo the damage caused by the people's sins. For that a greater king would be needed. Now Christ, the true vine, has come, and we receive life from our attachment to him. Because of him we can pray, "Restore us, O Lord God Almighty; make your face shine upon us, that we may be saved" (verse 19).

# Psalm 81

### *If only*

A saying goes, "Of all the sad words of tongue and pen the saddest are these: It might have been." The most tragic thing about Israel's sad history is that it could have been so different. All the suffering that was causing so much distress to the psalmist was unnecessary. If only Israel had obeyed the Lord, how different its history would have been! The people could have remained in their land, loaded down with blessings. They could have waited for the Messiah's coming in joy and peace. But because they turned away from the Lord, their history was filled with war, bloodshed, and disaster. This psalm contrasts the joy of a festival in the Promised Land, which could have been the Israelites' permanent possession, with the grief that became theirs because of their disobedience. The psalm is based on Deuteronomy 5:29 and 32:29.

**For the director of music. According to *gittith*. Of Asaph.**

*Gittith* apparently refers to a musical instrument or a musical style that originated in the city of Gath.

*Invitation to worship*

¹ Sing for joy to God our strength;
shout aloud to the God of Jacob!
² Begin the music,
strike the tambourine,
play the melodious harp and lyre.
³ Sound the ram's horn at the New Moon,
and when the moon is full,
on the day of our Feast;

⁴ this is a decree for Israel,
an ordinance of the God of Jacob.
⁵ He established it as a statute for Joseph
when he went out against Egypt,
where we heard a language we did not understand.

⁶ He says, "I removed the burden from their shoulders;
their hands were set free from the basket.
⁷ In your distress you called and I rescued you,
I answered you out of a thundercloud;
I tested you at the waters of Meribah.          ***Selah***

Israel is invited to join in the worship at one of the festivals that celebrated its delivery from slavery in Egypt. This psalm seems most appropriate to the Feast of Tabernacles, at which the Law was to be read every seventh year. The new moon, which marked the start of the seventh month, was celebrated with the blowing of the ram's horn. The full moon, on the 15th day of the seventh month, marked the beginning of the Feast of Tabernacles.

The Holy Land was given to the Israelites as a place in which they would be free to worship God and enjoy the fruits with which he had blessed them. This psalm echoes the theme of Deuteronomy, in which the Israelites are admonished not to forget the blessings of God, but to honor him with thanksgiving.

The following section warns of the consequences of refusing this invitation to worship. This same contrast of worship and warning occurs in Psalm 95.

## *Warning against idolatry*

> [8] **"Hear, O my people, and I will warn you—**
> **if you would but listen to me, O Israel!**
>
> [9] **You shall have no foreign god among you;**
> **you shall not bow down to an alien god.**
> [10] **I am the LORD your God,**
> **who brought you up out of Egypt.**
> **Open wide your mouth and I will fill it.**

At the same time that Israel was invited to worship God, the people were also warned of the consequences of disobedience. The books of Deuteronomy and Leviticus conclude with blessings for obedience and curses for disobedience.

The Israelites' main motive for obeying God's command to worship only him was to be the love they had for him because of what he had done for them. However, God also encouraged them with promises of continued blessing. How tragic it was that Israel forgot the past blessings and threw away the future blessings by turning from the Lord to idols.

> ¹¹ **"But my people would not listen to me;**
> **Israel would not submit to me.**
>
> ¹² **So I gave them over to their stubborn hearts**
> **to follow their own devices.**
>
> ¹³ **"If my people would but listen to me,**
> **if Israel would follow my ways,**
> ¹⁴ **how quickly would I subdue their enemies**
> **and turn my hand against their foes!**
> ¹⁵ **Those who hate the LORD would cringe before him,**
> **and their punishment would last forever.**
> ¹⁶ **But you would be fed with the finest of wheat;**
> **with honey from the rock I would satisfy you."**

The people of Israel chose the curses instead of the blessings. Instead of victory they received defeat. Instead of plenty they received famine. Instead of life they received death. This occurred again and again throughout the history of the Israelites as God sent various oppressors against them. This tragic situation reached a low point in the Babylonian captivity of 586 B.C. and again at the destruction of the temple by the Romans in A.D. 70.

The sad history of Israel is a warning to us. If God sent terrible judgments against his chosen people when they became unfaithful, can we expect to be let off more leniently if we follow their example of ingratitude?

# Psalm 82

## *Woe to corrupt rulers*

Although the people of Israel as a whole were not guiltless, a great deal of the blame for the sad outcome of Israel's history falls on its corrupt rulers. They not only failed to provide good spiritual leadership for the people. They also exploited and oppressed the people in order to satisfy their own greed. The prophets Hosea, Amos, Isaiah, and Micah all sharply condemned such sins of the ruling class of Israel. Psalm 82 calls for judgment upon the corrupt rulers of Israel and upon all other rulers who abuse the trust God has given them.

**A psalm of Asaph.**

¹God presides in the great assembly;
he gives judgment among the "gods":
²"How long will you defend the unjust
and show partiality to the wicked?                    *Selah*

³ Defend the cause of the weak and fatherless;
maintain the rights of the poor and oppressed.
⁴Rescue the weak and needy;
deliver them from the hand of the wicked.

⁵ "They know nothing, they understand nothing.
They walk about in darkness;
all the foundations of the earth are shaken.

⁶ "I said, 'You are "gods";
you are all sons of the Most High.'
⁷But you will die like mere men;
you will fall like every other ruler."

⁸ Rise up, O God, judge the earth,
for all the nations are your inheritance.

A widow and her children

The rulers are called "gods" because they are God's representatives and receive their power from him. Jesus refers to this psalm in John 10:34, when he is arguing with the leaders of the Jews because they were angry that he called himself the Son of God. Jesus' point in quoting Psalm 82 was this: If Scripture called God's earthly representatives "gods" (and every word of Scripture is inspired by God), why should the Jews be upset if God's true Son from heaven, his greatest representative to the human race, called himself "Son of God"?

The God-given responsibility of rulers is to punish the guilty and protect the good. All too often the rulers of Israel were doing just the opposite. When rulers ignore even the natural knowledge of God's law and lead their people into moral darkness, they destroy the very foundations of society. Rulers who so shamefully abuse the trust that God has given them will be judged most severely. Like the rulers of Israel, the rulers of our day who persecute the innocent and who tolerate such sins as abortion and immorality will have to answer to God for their negligence.

# Psalm 83

### *Surrounded by enemies*

Psalm 83 provides an apt conclusion to Asaph's collection, which deals with the distress of Israel. In it we see Israel surrounded by enemies and dependent on God for rescue. If written by the Asaph of David's day, as seems probable, it is a general psalm applicable to any point of Israel's history. In it the enemies from Israel's early days serve as representatives of all the enemies of God's people. A similar usage occurs in Revelation chapter 18, in which the great enemy of God's people during the New Testament era is called

Babylon, the name of their great enemy in Old Testament times. A historical occasion to which this psalm is especially appropriate is the invasion of Judah by Moab, Ammon, and Edom, recorded in 2 Chronicles chapter 20. Israel's victory on that occasion was foretold by Jahaziel, a descendant of Asaph (2 Chronicles 20:14).

**A song. A psalm of Asaph.**

## *Opening plea*

> ¹**O God, do not keep silent;**
> **be not quiet, O God, be not still.**

In this very brief opening prayer, the psalmist calls on God to come to Israel's rescue. He follows this plea with a catalog of Israel's enemies and their crimes.

## *Catalog of enemies*

> ²**See how your enemies are astir,**
> **how your foes rear their heads.**
> ³**With cunning they conspire against your people;**
> **they plot against those you cherish.**
> ⁴**"Come," they say, "let us destroy them as a nation,**
> **that the name of Israel be remembered no more."**
> ⁵**With one mind they plot together;**
> **they form an alliance against you—**
> > ⁶**the tents of Edom and the Ishmaelites,**
> > **of Moab and the Hagrites,**
> > ⁷**Gebal, Ammon and Amalek,**
> > **Philistia, with the people of Tyre.**
> > ⁸**Even Assyria has joined them**
> > > **to lend strength to the descendants of Lot.**
> > > ***Selah***

The Edomites were descendants of Esau who lived south-east of the Dead Sea. The Ishmaelites, who lived south of

Israel, and perhaps also the Hagrites, were descendants of Abraham's son Ishmael. The Hagrites are mentioned in 1 Chronicles chapter 5 as enemies of the tribe of Reuben, who lived east of the Jordan during the time of Saul. The Amalekites also lived mainly to the south of Israel. The Moabites and Ammonites were descendants of Lot who lived east of the Jordan. The Philistines were Israel's enemies on the west. The people of Gebal and Tyre were Canaanite-Phoenicians who lived north of Israel. (The NIV understands Gebal as the Phoenician city of Byblos, located in present-day Lebanon. Because of its position in the text, some commentators believe it is a more obscure Gebal, located near Edom.) Thus Israel is completely surrounded by enemies.

If this psalm was written by the Asaph of David's day, the mention of Assyria is somewhat surprising, since it was not a factor until late in Israel's history, and the nations mentioned as enemies of Israel in this psalm were generally enemies of Assyria, not its allies. Since "Asshur," the Hebrew name of Assyria, is also the name of a small nation in the southern regions inhabited by the Amalekites and Ishmaelites (Genesis 25:3,18), it is possible that the NIV translators have misunderstood the text and should have translated verse 8, "Also Asshur has joined them." Like many of the other nations in this list, these southern Asshurites were related to Israel; they were descendants of Abraham's wife Keturah. In this context, a reference to the nearby southern Asshur seems more appropriate than a reference to the distant northern Assyria. It appears that the NIV translators made the same error in Numbers 24:22,24, since the Kittim in that section are probably the Philistines and the Asshurites, their southern neighbors.

### Prayer for destruction of the enemies

> **⁹Do to them as you did to Midian,**
> **as you did to Sisera and Jabin at the river Kishon,**

<sup>10</sup>who perished at Endor and became like refuse on the ground.
<sup>11</sup>Make their nobles like Oreb and Zeeb,
  all their princes like Zebah and Zalmunna,
<sup>12</sup>who said, "Let us take possession
      of the pasturelands of God."
<sup>13</sup>Make them like tumbleweed, O my God,
  like chaff before the wind.
<sup>14</sup>As fire consumes the forest
  or a flame sets the mountains ablaze,
<sup>15</sup>so pursue them with your tempest
  and terrify them with your storm.
<sup>16</sup>Cover their faces with shame
      so that men will seek your name, O LORD.
<sup>17</sup>May they ever be ashamed and dismayed;
  may they perish in disgrace.
<sup>18</sup>Let them know that you, whose name is the LORD—
  that you alone are the Most High over all the earth.

In this section the psalmist prays that God will defeat the present and future enemies of Israel as decisively as he crushed and scattered its past enemies. Midian and its rulers, Oreb and Zeeb, Zebah and Zalmunna, were defeated by Gideon (Judges 7,8). Sisera was defeated by Deborah (Judges 4). These victories are appropriate examples of divine intervention on the people of Israel's behalf, since they so clearly depended on the grace and power of God, not on the strength or courage of Israel's army. The comparisons to tumbleweeds and chaff, fire and storm, emphasize the completeness of the enemies' defeat.

The goals of the psalmist's prayer are set forth in verses 16 and 18—the glory of God and the repentance of his enemies are the psalmist's chief concerns. The psalmist's motivation is also brought out in verses 2 to 4. He must regard these people as his enemies because they are God's enemies. They oppose God's plan and try to rob his people of their inheritance. In every age God's people are to pray: "Hallowed be your name. Your kingdom come. Your will be done." This was Asaph's prayer in his day. It must be our prayer also. Today when the church is surrounded by so many enemies we pray, "O God, do not keep silent; be not quiet, O God, be not still" (verse 1).

# The psalms of the sons of Korah
# (Psalms 84–89)

The rest of Book 3 of Psalms consists of psalms of the sons of Korah, except for Psalm 86, which is a psalm of David. The sons of Korah were a group of Levitical singers descended from the Korah who rebelled against Moses. Psalms 42 to 49 in Book 2 are also by the sons of Korah. Both of these groups of psalms contrast the joy the psalmist finds in God's house in Jerusalem with the sorrow of being separated from God. In the first group of Korahite psalms, the name God predominates, but the name Lord predominates in this group of psalms.

# Psalm 84

### *How lovely is your dwelling place*

Psalm 84, which emphasizes the joy of being in God's house, provides an excellent introduction to this group of psalms.

**For the director of music. According to *gittith*.**
**Of the Sons of Korah. A psalm.**

*Gittith* apparently refers to a musical instrument or style of music developed in the city of Gath.

¹How lovely is your dwelling place, O LORD Almighty!
²My soul yearns, even faints,
　　　for the courts of the LORD;
　my heart and my flesh cry out for the living God.

³Even the sparrow has found a home,
　and the swallow a nest for herself,
　　　where she may have her young—
　　　a place near your altar,
　O LORD Almighty, my King and my God.

⁴Blessed are those who dwell in your house;
　they are ever praising you.　　　　　　　　　　*Selah*
⁵Blessed are those whose strength is in you,
　who have set their hearts on pilgrimage.
⁶As they pass through the Valley of Baca,
　they make it a place of springs;
　the autumn rains also cover it with pools.
⁷They go from strength to strength,
　till each appears before God in Zion.

⁸Hear my prayer, O LORD God Almighty;
　listen to me, O God of Jacob.　　　　　　　　*Selah*
⁹Look upon our shield, O God;
　look with favor on your anointed one.

¹⁰Better is one day in your courts
　　　than a thousand elsewhere;
　I would rather be a doorkeeper in the house of my God
　　　than dwell in the tents of the wicked.

¹¹For the LORD God is a sun and shield;
　the LORD bestows favor and honor;
　no good thing does he withhold
　　　from those whose walk is blameless.
¹²O LORD Almighty, blessed is the man
　　　who trusts in you.

The intense longing for God's house that is expressed in
this psalm is very similar to that expressed in Psalms 42 and

43. It appears that war or some other circumstances are making it impossible for the psalmist to join in the pilgrimages to Jerusalem for the religious festivals. Even birds who build their nests in the eaves of the temple have access to God's house, but the psalmist is excluded.

*Baca* means "balsam tree," but no real geographic place named the Valley of Baca or Balsam Valley is known in the land of Israel. Therefore the "Valley of Baca" may be a figurative allusion to the psalmist's sorrow, since in Hebrew it sounds like the "valley of sorrow."

Although there may be a hint of sorrow, this psalm is predominantly joyful. If the psalmist is cut off from God's house, his joy as he contemplates restoration to God's house overwhelms the distress of any temporary separation. Throughout the psalm he speaks of the joy and strength of those who worship in God's house. The pools of the Valley of Baca are symbols of spiritual blessing, because the Hebrew word for *pools* sounds like the word for *blessing*.

The word "blessed," or "happy," occurs three times in the psalm. Each time there is a stronger expression of peace and satisfaction. In verse 3 there is a wistful longing to join the pilgrims in Jerusalem. In verse 2 there is determination to make the journey. In verse 12 there are confidence and contentment. If the Lord withholds no good thing from those who trust in him, he will surely not withhold the best thing of all—the joy of worshiping in his presence.

The "shield" for whom the psalmist prays (verse 9) is probably the king, on whom the nation's safety depended so heavily.

During the Old Testament, the full joy of worshiping God was possible only in one city and in one building, because the sacrifices could be offered only in the temple of Jerusalem. Today our worship is not limited to any one place. We are free to worship God anywhere.

Nevertheless, our churches hold special places in our hearts. There we have been baptized, confirmed, and married. There we have witnessed these events in the lives of our loved ones. There we have heard words of comfort at the deaths of family members and friends. From those pulpits we have heard God's Word. At that altar we have received Christ's true body and blood, which were given and shed for our forgiveness. We too can say, "How lovely is your dwelling place, O LORD Almighty" (verse 1). It is true that we can worship God anywhere, but may we never, through our own negligence or indifference, deprive ourselves of the joy of joining fellow believers in God's house.

# Psalm 85

### *You showed favor to your land*

Psalm 85 has the same blend of joy and sorrow as Psalm 84. It rejoices in God's past goodness to his people, but it implies that this goodness is not being fully experienced in the present.

Some commentators have suggested that the past restoration referred to in this psalm is the return from the exile in Babylon and that the present distress refers to the troubles the people of Judah experienced during the time of Ezra and Nehemiah. This interpretation rests in part on the fact that the second half of verse 1 may be translated, "You returned Jacob from captivity." This interpretation is followed by the King James Version.

According to the NIV interpretation, "You restored the fortunes of Jacob," this psalm need not be a reference to postexilic times but could refer to almost any time of distress during Israel's history. It seems most likely that the past goodness refers to the many times of relief God had given Israel during the days of the judges and kings and that the present distress refers especially to the captivity in Babylon. This, of course, does not rule out prophetic authorship long before the time of the exile.

**For the director of music. Of the Sons of Korah. A psalm.**

*Past goodness*

**¹You showed favor to your land, O LORD;**
**you restored the fortunes of Jacob.**
**²You forgave the iniquity of your people**
**and covered all their sins.**                    *Selah*
**³You set aside all your wrath**
**and turned from your fierce anger.**

The psalmist recognized that the Israelites' past troubles had been a result of their sin. Their restoration, therefore, was an assurance that their sins had been forgiven, just as Jesus' healing of the crippled man was a sign that his sins had been forgiven (Mark 2:10,11).

*Present distress*

**⁴Restore us again, O God our Savior,**
**and put away your displeasure toward us.**
**⁵Will you be angry with us forever?**
**Will you prolong your anger**
**through all generations?**
**⁶Will you not revive us again,**
**that your people may rejoice in you?**

This part of the psalm echoes the theme of Psalm 74. Like that psalm, it seems to be aimed at Israel's most devastating experience, the captivity in Babylon. Since God does not operate on whims, but according to the unchangeable principle of grace expressed in the gospel, the psalmist is confident that Israel will again experience the same mercy it had experienced so often in the past.

*Hope for the future*

⁷Show us your unfailing love, O LORD,
  and grant us your salvation.

⁸I will listen to what God the LORD will say;
  he promises peace to his people, his saints—
  but let them not return to folly.

⁹Surely his salvation is near those who fear him,
  that his glory may dwell in our land.
¹⁰Love and faithfulness meet together;
  righteousness and peace kiss each other.
¹¹Faithfulness springs forth from the earth,
  and righteousness looks down from heaven.
¹²The LORD will indeed give what is good,
  and our land will yield its harvest.
¹³Righteousness goes before him
  and prepares the way for his steps.

This section of Psalm 85 is noteworthy for its picturesque language. The blessings the Lord provides are portrayed as people who meet with a kiss and as crops that spring up and flourish. Although this promise was fulfilled in a limited way when God restored Israel from captivity, this section is best understood as a description of the blessings of the messianic era.

God's glory was dwelling in the land of Israel when Christ came and lived there (Haggai 2:7-9; John 1:14). The peace and righteousness in this psalm are not political. They are the peace and righteousness won for us by Christ. The harvest of the land is not agricultural. It is the gathering of people into the Israel made up of all who believe.

The harmony that existed between heaven and earth at creation was restored when the barrier of sin that excluded us from paradise was removed by Christ. This division between heaven and earth will be completely removed when Christ returns and we live together in the new heavens and new earth (Revelation 21). The worldwide preaching of Christ's righteousness is now preparing the way for his return. Then the fulfillment of this psalm will be complete.

The blessings enumerated in this section are the blessings of the gospel, but verse 8—let his saints "not return to folly"—reminds us that the free blessings of the gospel should never be misused as an excuse for sinning. Because we are preparing for life in the new heavens and a new earth, where perfect righteousness dwells, we strive to do God's will on earth, even as it is done in heaven. We are eager for the day when we will live in true righteousness in heaven.

# Psalm 86

### *Guard my life*

As the only psalm of David in Book 3 of Psalms, Psalm 86 seems strangely out of place. However, it does have some thematic connections with the psalms that surround it. Its plea for deliverance and its emphasis on forgiveness echo Psalm 85. The reference to the gathering of the nations in verse 9 points ahead to Psalm 87.

The opening sections of the psalm set forth David's plea and its foundations.

**A prayer of David.**

*David's need, David's faith*
> ¹**Hear, O Lord, and answer me,**
> **for I am poor and needy.**

²Guard my life,
>for I am devoted to you.
>You are my God;
save your servant
>who trusts in you.
³Have mercy on me, O Lord,
>for I call to you all day long.
⁴Bring joy to your servant,
>for to you, O Lord, I lift up my soul.

## God's grace

⁵You are forgiving and good, O Lord,
abounding in love to all who call to you.
⁶Hear my prayer, O Lord;
listen to my cry for mercy.

## God's ruling power

⁷In the day of my trouble I will call to you,
>for you will answer me.
⁸Among the gods there is none like you, O Lord;
no deeds can compare with yours.
⁹All the nations you have made will come
and worship before you, O Lord;
they will bring glory to your name.
¹⁰For you are great and do marvelous deeds;
you alone are God.

In the first section, the indentation indicates the interweaving of David's plea with statements of his need and of his faith. Five times David calls on the Lord for help. Each of these five pleas for help is followed by an expression of the psalmist's need and his faithfulness in seeking help from the Lord (the indented lines). The characteristics of the psalmist that should move God to hear his prayer are emphasized in this opening section.

In the second and third sections of the plea, David moves on to a surer foundation for his prayer, namely, the attributes of God that provide David with the confidence to pray. The second section emphasizes the love and mercy of God, which move him to forgive our sins. The third section proclaims the power of God, by which he controls all things for the good of his people. David looks forward to the day when not only a remnant of Israel but people from all nations will recognize God's grace and power and will come to him.

A special emphasis on the power of God may be indicated by the fact that the name Lord in this psalm is often the Hebrew word for *master* (written *Lord* in the English Bible) rather than *Yahweh*, the covenant name of God (written *Lord* in the English Bible).

"Among the gods there is none like you" (verse 8) does not imply an acceptance of polytheism any more than the First Commandment does (Exodus 20:3). It simply recognizes that there are many so-called gods in the world whom people serve in their blindness. None of them are real, however. They are products of human imagination and Satan's delusions. This is clearly stated in verse 10: "You alone are God."

### *The praise*

<sup>11</sup>Teach me your way, O Lord,
   and I will walk in your truth;
   give me an undivided heart,
   that I may fear your name.

<sup>12</sup>I will praise you, O Lord my God,
         with all my heart;
   I will glorify your name forever.
<sup>13</sup>For great is your love toward me;
   you have delivered me from the depths
         of the grave.

In the middle portion of this psalm, David expresses his confidence that God will answer his prayer. When he is delivered from death, he will praise and thank God from an undivided heart. He recognizes that he will be able to fulfill this promise only if the Lord creates such an undivided heart within him through the power of his Word.

*The plea repeated*

<sup>14</sup>**The arrogant are attacking me, O God;**
**a band of ruthless men seeks my life—**
**men without regard for you.**

<sup>15</sup> **But you, O Lord, are a compassionate**
**and gracious God,**
**slow to anger, abounding in love and faithfulness.**

<sup>16</sup> **Turn to me and have mercy on me;**
**grant your strength to your servant**
**and save the son of your maidservant.**

<sup>17</sup> **Give me a sign of your goodness,**
**that my enemies may see it and be put to shame,**
**for you, O LORD, have helped me and comforted me.**

The crisis has apparently not yet passed, since David repeats his plea. Such repetition of prayer is not a demonstration of weakness of faith; it is, rather, an example of the persistence in prayer that Jesus urged upon his followers (Luke 18:1-5).

It is a mark of David's restraint that he holds back the description of his enemies this far into the prayer. His first focus is on God's attributes and his glory. The enemies of David are probably either the supporters of Saul or the co-conspirators of Absalom.

The beautiful description of the Lord in verse 15 is one of Israel's favorite descriptions of the gracious God. It originates in God's proclamation to Moses in Exodus 34:6 and is repeated many times in the Old Testament.

God has compassionate feelings for his people like those a mother has for her child, in spite of her faults and weaknesses. He has generosity like that of a father who freely gives undeserved, unearned gifts to his children. He has patience like that of a parent who again and again instructs a child in the right way. God is faithful to the promises he has made in the gospel. He will never abandon them.

David closes with this prayer: "Hallowed be your name." When David is delivered, it will be clear to all that God is ruling and that his will cannot be overturned. When David is helped and comforted, the plan of Satan's allies will have come to nothing, and God will be glorified.

# Psalm 87

## *The glorious city*

Like Psalms 47 and 67, Psalm 87 expresses a world mission theme. It declares the same love for God's Holy City as Psalms 48 and 122. The hymn "Glorious Things of Thee Are Spoken" is based on this psalm. It introduces a bright ray of hope into this section of psalms by looking to the glorious future of Jerusalem.

*The Holy City*

**Of the Sons of Korah. A psalm. A song.**

¹ **He has set his foundation on the holy mountain;**
² **the LORD loves the gates of Zion**
    **more than all the dwellings of Jacob.**
³ **Glorious things are said of you, O city of God:**

                                                                     *Selah*

⁴ "I will record Rahab and Babylon
     among those who acknowledge me—
Philistia too, and Tyre, along with Cush—
     and will say, 'This one was born in Zion.'"
⁵ Indeed, of Zion it will be said,
  "This one and that one were born in her,
  and the Most High himself will establish her."
⁶ The LORD will write in the register of the peoples:
  "This one was born in Zion."

                                                        **Selah**

⁷ As they make music they will sing,
  "All my fountains are in you."

Although it does not mention the temple, this psalm is obviously based on the fact that the Lord's temple was built on Mount Zion in Jerusalem. The presence of the temple made Jerusalem a unique city on the earth. However, like the other psalms that glorify Jerusalem, this psalm looks beyond the earthly city to the spiritual Jerusalem, which is the church on earth, and to the heavenly Jerusalem, the church in heaven. God has only one chosen people in the full sense of the term, that is, his spiritual Israel made up of all who believe in the Messiah, regardless of whether they are Jews or Gentiles by birth.

Gentiles, who were enemies of God and of his people, become citizens of Israel through faith in Christ. Citizenship in the true Israel, which will inherit God's promises, does not depend on physical descent but on spiritual rebirth. This truth is taught many places in the New Testament.

One of the fullest statements is found in Ephesians 2:1-20, which includes Paul's declaration to the Ephesians, "You are no longer foreigners and aliens, but fellow citizens with God's people and members of God's household, built on the foundation of the apostles and prophets, with Christ Jesus himself as the chief cornerstone." Similar statements are found in Romans 4:16 and 11:13-24 and in many other passages.

Rahab is a name for Egypt, and Cush is the region south of Egypt. Together with Babylon they represent the great enemies of Israel during the Old Testament. Philistia and Tyre represent enemies closer to home. This prophecy was fulfilled literally when inhabitants of all these countries came to faith through the ministry of the apostles after Pentecost. However, these names represent all of the people from all nations who come to faith throughout the New Testament era.

By nature we too were enemies of God and his people, but through Baptism we were made his children by faith in Christ Jesus. We have become Abraham's children through faith in Abraham's promised seed (Galatians 3:26-29).

The alternate translation offered in the NIV footnote, "O Rahab and Babylon, Philistia, Tyre and Cush, I will record concerning those who acknowledge me: 'This one was born in Zion,'" seems to be a taunt to the enemies, which lessens the mission emphasis of this psalm. There is nothing in the psalm itself or in the larger context of Scripture to make this alternative rendering preferable to the rendering in the main text of the NIV. The theme of world missions occurs often in the Old Testament, especially in Isaiah, so it should be retained here as well.

This is a psalm of God's grace. Because of God's love and his choice, the Holy City becomes God's special possession. Because of his proclamation, even his enemies are called to enter the Holy City. It is due to his grace alone that the kings of the earth enter his city and drink of the fountains of life (Revelation 21:22–22:21).

# Psalm 88

## *Darkness is my friend*

Psalm 88 is one of the most unusual psalms, both in its literary background and in its theme. It is the only psalm with a double heading.

**A song. A psalm of the Sons of Korah. For the director of music.**
**According to *mahalath leannoth*. A *maskil* of Heman the Ezrahite.**

The caption "For the director of music" is normally found at the beginning of a psalm heading, so it is likely that this phrase is the dividing point between the two captions. The content of the first heading is identical with that of Psalm 87. For that reason some commentators suggest that the first heading really belongs at the end of Psalm 87 and that it was misplaced when it was attached to Psalm 88.

However, the Levitical singer Heman was a member of the sons of Korah. He was also a grandson of the prophet Samuel (1 Chronicles 6:33-37). It is therefore probable that the first heading *does* belong with Psalm 88 and that the second heading is an elaboration of the first. However, the problem is complicated by the fact that there was another Heman, who was known for his wisdom. He was from the tribe of Judah and the family of Zerah (1 Kings 4:31; 1 Chronicles 2:6). This would offer a possible explanation for the term "Ezrahite," but a member of the tribe of Judah would not be among the temple musicians. It seems most likely that the author of this psalm is the Levitical Heman and that the term "Ezrahite" refers to his place of residence.

Another possibility proposed by some commentators is that the two Hemans are really the same person and that he is classified as a Levite by descent and a Judean by residence. This is a possibility, since Samuel's father is listed both as a

Levite and an Ephraimite on the basis of descent and resi-dence (1 Samuel 1:1; 1 Chronicles 6:34).

If both headings belong to this psalm, the psalm has three different designations: "psalm," "song," and *"maskil."* A *maskil* is a skillful psalm or an instructive psalm. The term *mahalath leannoth* appears only in this psalm and seems to mean "the suffering of affliction." If so, it is very fitting for this psalm. It may be the title of the tune or the style of music to which the psalm is to be performed. The title *mahalath* appears with Psalm 53.

The content of this psalm is also unusual in that the only spark of hope is in verse 1, which refers to the God who saves. The rest of the psalm is unrelieved darkness. Even the end of the psalm offers no hope for the future but ends in gloom. This is even more striking in the Hebrew, in which the last word is *darkness.*

> [1] **O LORD, the God who saves me,**
>    **day and night I cry out before you.**
> [2] **May my prayer come before you;**
>    **turn your ear to my cry.**
>
> [3] **For my soul is full of trouble**
>    **and my life draws near the grave.**
> [4] **I am counted among those who go down to the pit;**
>    **I am like a man without strength.**
> [5] **I am set apart with the dead,**
>    **like the slain who lie in the grave,**
>    **whom you remember no more,**
>    **who are cut off from your care.**
> [6] **You have put me in the lowest pit,**
>    **in the darkest depths.**
> [7] **Your wrath lies heavily upon me;**
>    **you have overwhelmed me with all your waves.**
>
> ***Selah***

⁸You have taken from me my closest friends
and have made me repulsive to them.
I am confined and cannot escape;
⁹my eyes are dim with grief.
I call to you, O LORD, every day;
I spread out my hands to you.

¹⁰Do you show your wonders to the dead?
Do those who are dead rise up and praise you?

*Selah*

¹¹Is your love declared in the grave,
your faithfulness in Destruction?
¹²Are your wonders known in the place of darkness,
or your righteous deeds in the land of oblivion?

¹³But I cry to you for help, O LORD;
in the morning my prayer comes before you.

¹⁴Why, O LORD, do you reject me
and hide your face from me?

¹⁵From my youth I have been afflicted
and close to death;
I have suffered your terrors
and am in despair.
¹⁶Your wrath has swept over me;
your terrors have destroyed me.
¹⁷All day long they surround me like a flood;
they have completely engulfed me.
¹⁸You have taken my companions
and loved ones from me;
the darkness is my closest friend.

"My soul is full of trouble" aptly summarizes this psalm. The danger of death, an awareness of God's wrath, a failure to see any possible reason for his affliction, and the loss of family and friends are among the woes that overwhelm Heman.

There are two special problems raised by the content of this psalm. The first is the depth of Heman's despair. It is shocking to many readers, who can imagine such words coming only from an unbeliever. But God's children too may find themselves temporarily overcome by despair when devastating disaster strikes them. Job and Jeremiah were two other believers who passed through the same depths as Heman did before they regained their spiritual bearings. Asaph, the author of Psalm 73, was also near the brink.

Such despair is not right, nor is it necessary, since the good and powerful God is still in control even when the situation looks dark. But God has allowed such dark hours of his saints to be recorded in the Scriptures for our benefit. Though their faith was hanging on by a thread, God did not allow the thread to be broken. God does not break the bruised reed or snuff out the smoldering wick of faith (Matthew 12:20). He will bind up the broken reed and fan the faint spark of faith into a flame again.

This psalm is written for our benefit, so that if we ever face times as dark as those of Heman, we will recognize that we are not unique in our anguish. Like Heman, we can cling to the dim spark of faith and can continue to pray until God makes the answers clear to us once again.

There may even be some cases for which we never learn the *why* or from which we never gain relief in this life. If so, we must endure until God removes us from this life. We will refuse to accept the present distress as God's final word to us, and we will continue to pray even in the darkness.

The second problem raised by the content of this psalm is the seeming denial of life after death in verses 10 through 12. Similar thoughts appear in some of the psalms of

David, such as Psalm 6. These psalms are viewing the issue only from the point of view of earthly life. From that perspective it is true that we will never come this way again. It is true that this life is our one opportunity to receive and to share the gospel.

Therefore Heman is asking for relief from his afflictions, since such relief will serve as a sign of God's love and will demonstrate the faithfulness of his promises. Such relief will also strengthen Heman and others, and it will restore Heman's ability to serve God on this earth. Although Psalm 88 ends on a jarring note, Psalm 89 will point to the relief for which Heman longs.

# Psalm 89

## *You promised David*

Psalm 89 is an appropriate companion to Psalm 88. The question of authorship posed by the heading of Psalm 89 is closely related to that raised by the heading of Psalm 88. Heman the Levitical musician had an associate named Ethan, and Heman of Judah had a brother named Ethan, so the same twofold possibility concerning authorship that was discussed in the opening comments to Psalm 88 applies here. This Ethan could be either the Levitical temple musician or the wise man of Judah, or the two may be one and the same person.

These two psalms are also closely related in theme, since both of them deal with the distress of God's people. The major difference is that Psalm 89 provides some relief to the deep gloom of Psalm 88. Psalm 89 ends with an unanswered question, but it has a brighter tone than Psalm 88, since its opening praise is more emphatic and more confident than the opening of Psalm 88. Psalm 89 also has a much more detailed exposition of the promises and power of God.

**A *maskil* of Ethan the Ezrahite.**

*Opening praise*

> [1] **I will sing of the L**ord**'s great love forever;**
> **with my mouth I will make your faithfulness known**
> **through all generations.**
> [2] **I will declare that your love stands firm forever,**
> **that you established your faithfulness**
> **in heaven itself.**

In the opening praise, Ethan sets the tone for the whole psalm by firmly declaring his confidence in God's faithfulness to the covenant promises he has made with Israel. Although Ethan is going to raise some questions about the way God is demonstrating that faithfulness, he asks his questions with the same willingness to learn as Mary, who asked, "How will this be?" (Luke 1:34). He asks with the same longing for reassurance shown by John the Baptist. John sent messengers to question Jesus because it was hard for him and his disciples to believe that Jesus could really be the promised Messiah if he was going to leave John sitting in Herod's prison (Matthew 11:1-14).

Ethan moves from his general statement of faith to the specific problem that is bothering him. In 2 Samuel 7:4-17 God had promised David that one of David's heirs would remain on his throne forever. How could this promise be reconciled with the partial loss of David's kingdom brought about by the secession and the eventual collapse of the northern kingdom of Israel? How could it be harmonized with the complete downfall of the Davidic rule, which occurred when Jerusalem fell to the Babylonians? If Jehoiachin, the heir to the throne of Judah, was an exile in Babylon, how could God's promise that David's heir would rule forever come true? (If this psalm was written by the Ethan of

David's day, it was written in prophetic anticipation of the schism of the north and the fall of Judah.)

Ethan's review of the covenant with David has five main parts, which are indicated by the paragraphs of the following section.

## The covenant with David

### 1. Statement of the covenant

³ You said, "I have made a covenant
  with my chosen one,
I have sworn to David my servant,
⁴ 'I will establish your line forever
and make your throne firm
        through all generations.'"            **Selah**

### 2. God's power, which upholds the covenant

⁵ The heavens praise your wonders, O LORD,
  your faithfulness too, in the assembly
        of the holy ones.
⁶ For who in the skies above can compare
        with the LORD?
  Who is like the LORD among the heavenly beings?
⁷ In the council of the holy ones
    God is greatly feared;
  he is more awesome than all who surround him.
⁸ O LORD God Almighty, who is like you?
  You are mighty, O LORD,
  and your faithfulness surrounds you.
⁹ You rule over the surging sea;
  when its waves mount up, you still them.
¹⁰ You crushed Rahab like one of the slain;
  with your strong arm you scattered your enemies.
¹¹ The heavens are yours, and yours also the earth;
  you founded the world and all that is in it.

¹² You created the north and the south;
    Tabor and Hermon sing for joy at your name.
¹³ Your arm is endued with power;
    your hand is strong, your right hand exalted.
¹⁴ Righteousness and justice are the foundation
        of your throne;
    love and faithfulness go before you.

### 3. *The security of God's people*

¹⁵ Blessed are those who have learned to acclaim you,
    who walk in the light of your presence, O LORD.
¹⁶ They rejoice in your name all day long;
    they exult in your righteousness.
¹⁷ For you are their glory and strength,
    and by your favor you exalt our horn.
¹⁸ Indeed, our shield belongs to the LORD,
    our king to the Holy One of Israel.

### 4. *The promise to David*

¹⁹ Once you spoke in a vision,
    to your faithful people you said:
    "I have bestowed strength on a warrior;
    I have exalted a young man from
        among the people.
²⁰ I have found David my servant;
    with my sacred oil I have anointed him.
²¹ My hand will sustain him;
    surely my arm will strengthen him.
²² No enemy will subject him to tribute;
    no wicked man will oppress him.
²³ I will crush his foes before him
    and strike down his adversaries.
²⁴ My faithful love will be with him,
    and through my name his horn will be exalted.

²⁵ I will set his hand over the sea,
   his right hand over the rivers.
²⁶ He will call out to me, 'You are my Father,
   my God, the Rock my Savior.'
²⁷ I will also appoint him my firstborn,
   the most exalted of the kings of the earth.
²⁸ I will maintain my love to him forever,
   and my covenant with him will never fail.
²⁹ I will establish his line forever,
   his throne as long as the heavens endure.

## 5. *The terms of the covenant*

³⁰ "If his sons forsake my law
      and do not follow my statutes,
³¹ if they violate my decrees
      and fail to keep my commands,
³² I will punish their sin with the rod,
      their iniquity with flogging;
³³ but I will not take my love from him,
   nor will I ever betray my faithfulness.
³⁴ I will not violate my covenant
   or alter what my lips have uttered.
³⁵ Once for all, I have sworn by my holiness—
   and I will not lie to David—
³⁶ that his line will continue forever
   and his throne endure before me like the sun;
³⁷ it will be established forever like the moon,
   the faithful witness in the sky."

**Selah**

The first paragraph briefly summarizes the promise: an heir of David will rule on his throne forever.

The second and third paragraphs state two general principles that bolster the psalmist's faith in the fulfillment of the promise. God has shown his power to fulfill his promise by his rule over all creation. God rules over the angels he created. He rules over the sea, which no man can tame. Rahab is a figurative name for the sea, a monster that only God can control. God rules over the highest mountains. Tabor and Hermon were two of the most majestic mountains the Israelites knew. God's control of these three creations of his—angels, seas, and mountains—represents his power over all creation. Since he has such power, he can certainly fulfill his promise to David.

The second paragraph demonstrates God's ability to fulfill his promise; the third paragraph shows his desire to keep his promise. He wants to give glory, strength, and power to his people. He therefore will give them a king who will be a shield protecting them from their enemies.

The fourth paragraph provides a more detailed statement of the promise to David. Its length is probably intended to express the depth of the psalmist's feeling about the covenant. It has some similarities to Psalm 72, which celebrates the eternal rule of David's heir.

The fifth paragraph, which states the terms of the covenant, already hints at the answer to the psalmist's question. Although the promise that David would have an heir who would rule forever was unconditional, there was a condition attached to the enjoyment of that promise by individual heirs of David. Unfaithfulness and disobedience disqualified a king from the privilege of ruling on David's throne. Ungodly kings like Jehoiachin, who was carried into exile, or like Zedekiah, who died in prison in Babylon, were receiving the punishment their apostasy deserved. The removal of such ungodly kings from the throne was not a breaking of God's promise, but a fulfilling of a part of it.

But if such kings were removed and the line of David was broken, how could God keep the promise that an heir of David would always reign on his throne?

## *The covenant abandoned?*

<sup>38</sup> But you have rejected, you have spurned,
   you have been very angry with your anointed one.
<sup>39</sup> You have renounced the covenant with your servant
   and have defiled his crown in the dust.
<sup>40</sup> You have broken through all his walls
   and reduced his strongholds to ruins.
<sup>41</sup> All who pass by have plundered him;
   he has become the scorn of his neighbors.
<sup>42</sup> You have exalted the right hand of his foes;
   you have made all his enemies rejoice.
<sup>43</sup> You have turned back the edge of his sword
   and have not supported him in battle.
<sup>44</sup> You have put an end to his splendor
   and cast his throne to the ground.
<sup>45</sup> you have cut short the days of his youth;
   you have covered him with a mantle of shame.

                                                    **Selah**


<sup>46</sup> How long, O LORD? Will you hide yourself forever?
   How long will your wrath burn like fire?
<sup>47</sup> Remember how fleeting is my life.
   For what futility you have created all men!
<sup>48</sup> What man can live and not see death,
   or save himself from the power of the grave?

                                                    **Selah**


<sup>49</sup> O Lord, where is your former great love,
   which in your faithfulness you swore to David?
<sup>50</sup> Remember, Lord, how your servant has been mocked,
   how I bear in my heart the taunts
          of all the nations,
<sup>51</sup> the taunts with which your enemies have mocked,
          O LORD,
   with which they have mocked every step
          of your anointed one.

The question "How long, O LORD?" was not answered during the lifetime of the psalmist nor during the lifetime of the exiles. Those who returned from exile to rebuild the temple saw only some faint foreshadowings of the answer. Even John the Baptist saw only the beginning of the answer. We, however, have been blessed to see the fulfillment of the promise to David, which kings and prophets longed to see.

We have seen how God's eternal Son came into the world as David's son. Like David, he was not a self-chosen king or usurper. He was chosen and anointed by God. But even during Christ's years on earth the humiliation and lowliness of the Davidic kings had not yet ended. The Son of David endured mockery and affliction. He too asked, "My God, my God, why have you forsaken me?" (Matthew 27:46).

But after suffering and dying to free his people from sin, death, and the devil, he rose from the dead and was exalted to rule with power at the right hand of God. Only Christ, the Son of David who was perfectly faithful and obedient to God's will, could fulfill this promise by ruling over the kingdom of Israel forever. He rebuilds God's temple, the church. He gathers people from the whole world into God's heavenly Jerusalem. When he returns to rule visibly, the question "How long, O LORD?" will be answered for every believer finally and completely.

*Closing doxology*

> [52] **Praise be to the LORD forever!**
> **Amen and Amen.**

This closing doxology is the doxology not merely for Psalm 89 but for the whole of Book 3. It brings both the psalm and the book to a triumphant end.

Samuel anointing David

# BOOK FOUR

## *Psalms 90–106*

Books 4 and 5 of Psalms are very similar in style and subject matter. Some commentators have suggested that the division between them is artificial, intended to create five books of psalms in order to form a parallel with the five books of Moses. In these two books of psalms, the poetic parallelism is less regular than in the preceding three books. The system used to arrange the psalms of Books 4 and 5 is quite different from that in the preceding three books. Authorship was an important element of classification in Books 1 to 3, but an author is listed for only 19 of the 61 psalms in Books 4 and 5. Groups of psalms of praise and thanksgiving are the main device used to divide Books 4 and 5 into sections. The name Lord predominates in both of these books.

Books 1 to 3 emphasize the problems faced by David and his dynasty, but Books 4 and 5 focus more on God's answer to their problems.

# Psalm 90

## *Teach us to number our days*

Psalm 90, the only psalm of Moses in the psalter, forms a fitting introduction to Book 4 of Psalms, since Moses and Israel's experiences in the wilderness are mentioned frequently in this book. Psalms 95, 99, 103, 105, and 106 all refer to Moses or the wilderness experience. A psalm reflecting on death was a fitting subject for Moses because death as a judgment of God was experienced in very dramatic ways during the wilderness years. As the 40 years came to an end, Moses himself was facing death outside the Promised Land because of his disobedience to God. Psalm 106, the concluding psalm of Book 4, sounds the same solemn note of judgment that is found in Psalm 90.

Psalm 90 focuses on death as a judgment upon sin, but it also points to the Lord as the one whose power extends beyond death. For this reason Psalm 90 is one of the psalms most frequently heard at funerals. Because it rejoices in God's timelessness, it is frequently used on New Year's Eve. Isaac Watts' well-known hymn "Our God, Our Help in Ages Past" is based on this psalm.

**A prayer of Moses the man of God.**

*God is eternal*

> [1] **Lord, you have been our dwelling place**
> **throughout all generations.**
> [2] **Before the mountains were born**
> **or you brought forth the earth and the world,**
> **from everlasting to everlasting you are God.**

The opening verses of the psalm briefly proclaim the eternity of God so that it may be contrasted with the mortality of mankind, which will be emphasized in the following section. The psalmist is not interested in a philosophical discussion of God's eternity, but in the practical application of God's eternity. Moses begins and ends the psalm with the assertion that the Lord is our God. God's eternity is not simply described as the opposite of our mortality; it is proclaimed as the answer to our mortality. Since God is immortal and eternal, he can be a dwelling place for his people throughout all generations.

Verse 4 in the next section shows that God's eternity is not just endless time but independence from time. For God "a day is like a thousand years, and a thousand years are like a day" (2 Peter 3:8). Though we suffer change and decay, God remains unchanged. Before the earth was created, as long as it endures, and after it is gone, God is always the same.

The next section is concerned not merely with human mortality but with the reason for death.

## Man is mortal

> <sup>3</sup> You turn men back to dust, saying,
> "Return to dust, O sons of men."
> <sup>4</sup> For a thousand years in your sight are
> like a day that has just gone by,
> or like a watch in the night.
>
> <sup>5</sup> You sweep men away in the sleep of death;
> they are like the new grass of the morning—
> <sup>6</sup> though in the morning it springs up new,
> by evening it is dry and withered.
>
> <sup>7</sup> We are consumed by your anger
> and terrified by your indignation.

⁸ **You have set our iniquities before you,**
 **our secret sins in the light of your presence.**
⁹ **All our days pass away under your wrath;**
 **we finish our years with a moan.**

¹⁰ **The length of our days is seventy years—**
 **or eighty, if we have the strength;**
 **yet their span is but trouble and sorrow,**
 **for they quickly pass, and we fly away.**

¹¹ **Who knows the power of your anger?**
 **For your wrath is as great as the fear**
 **that is due you.**

The real cause of death is not natural weakness, sickness, or human violence. All of these may be secondary causes, but the real cause of death is God's judgment against sin. God did not create man to die, but death has become our sentence. God had warned Adam that the consequence of disobedience would be death. Nevertheless, Adam and Eve disobeyed God, and so death came to them and to all of their descendants (Genesis 3–5; Romans 5). "The wages of sin is death" (Romans 6:23).

Death is the separation of body and soul. God returns the body to the ground from which he created it, and the soul returns to God, who made it (Ecclesiastes 12:7).

Because of sin the life span of human beings is short. Seventy or 80 years are not a long time compared with God's eternity or even compared with human history. Often human life is much shorter than 70 years. It can be snuffed out in an instant. Compared to what it could have been if Adam and Eve had obeyed God, the life of human beings is as fragile and short as the life of a flower, which blooms beautifully but soon withers.

Because of sin the lives of men are troubled. The sorrows and difficulties that sin has introduced into the world fill the whole span of human life. For those with spiritual insight, the evils of life are a daily reminder of the seriousness of sin and the greatness of God's anger against sin. Many people try to suppress this knowledge, but even when they push God's Word aside, the natural knowledge of God and his law bring feelings of guilt to the surface again. The result is that fear of death is natural to all people. The inescapable sense of guilt and persistent reminders of God's wrath leave sinners with no escape.

To many people God's wrath against sin seems unreasonable and excessive. But we do not yet know the full wrath of God. Only hell will reveal it. God's wrath against sin is proportionate to the seriousness of sin. Sin is an offense against a limitless, holy God. Sin therefore deserves limitless punishment. For the guilty sinner there is no escape—no escape except by the grace of God.

## Mortal man needs God's grace

$^{12}$Teach us to number our days aright,
   that we may gain a heart of wisdom.

$^{13}$Relent, O Lord! How long will it be?
   Have compassion on your servants.
$^{14}$Satisfy us in the morning
      with your unfailing love,
   that we may sing for joy and be glad all our days.
$^{15}$Make us glad for as many days
      as you have afflicted us,
   for as many years as we have seen trouble.
$^{16}$May your deeds be shown to your servants,
   your splendor to their children.
$^{17}$May the favor of the Lord our God rest upon us;
   establish the work of our hands for us—
   yes, establish the work of our hands.

Moses' closing prayer contains two main elements. The first is a plea for understanding and wisdom. As we daily observe death all around us, we are warned to make the most of this time of grace that God has given us, since death is inevitable. We are warned against being like the rich fool who accumulated treasure on earth but forgot about the needs of his soul (Luke 12:13-21). Since we have only one life and that one life is short, we should use it to gain the wisdom that comes from God. That wisdom is the message of the gospel, through which we gain forgiveness of sins and salvation (1 Corinthians 1:18–2:14).

The second part of the prayer is a plea for mercy. We do not deserve to have our lives prolonged, but we pray that God will give us the time and the wisdom to serve him faithfully on this earth. Such labor brings joy to all the days of our lives, even to life under the burdens of sin. Only the labor that we do for the gospel can produce fruits that will endure into eternity. We pray that God will establish and bless our labors for the gospel so that they will bear fruit for us, for our children, and for others, now and forever.

# Psalm 91

## *The shadow of your wings*

Psalms 90 and 91 are connected by references to God as a dwelling and a refuge (90:1; 91:9). Psalm 91, however, offers relief from the intensity of Psalm 90. In Psalm 90 believers feel the heat of God's wrath. In Psalm 91 they rest in the shade of his protection. The use of the ancient names of God, Most High and the Almighty, also serves to link this psalm with the times and writings of Moses.

A striking feature of this psalm is the shift of persons among "he," "I," and "you." In liturgical use it is possible to divide the psalm into a dialog between two speakers or choruses, but as originally composed, it was probably the expression of a single person. We will so interpret it here.

According to this interpretation, the psalmist first states the general principle that all who seek shelter in the Most High will find peace and safety in his protection. In verse 2 he confesses his own faith in this principle. Then in the main body of the psalm, he exhorts each of his readers to place his trust in God's protection.

### *The general principle*

> ¹ **He who dwells in the shelter of the Most High**
> **will rest in the shadow of the Almighty.**

### *Application to oneself*

> ² **I will say of the LORD,**
> **"He is my refuge and my fortress,**
> **my God, in whom I trust."**

### *Application to others*

> ³ **Surely he will save you from the fowler's snare**
> **and from the deadly pestilence.**
> ⁴ **He will cover you with his feathers,**
> **and under his wings you will find refuge;**
>
> **His faithfulness will be your shield and rampart.**
> ⁵ **You will not fear the terror of night,**
> **nor the arrow that flies by day,**
> ⁶ **nor the pestilence that stalks in the darkness,**
> **nor the plague that destroys at midday.**
> ⁷ **A thousand may fall at your side,**
> **ten thousand at your right hand,**
> **but it will not come near you.**

⁸You will only observe with your eyes
and see the punishment of the wicked.

⁹If you make the Most High your dwelling—
even the LORD, who is my refuge—
¹⁰then no harm will befall you,
no disaster will come near your tent.
¹¹For he will command his angels concerning you
to guard you in all your ways;
¹²they will lift you up in their hands,
so that you will not strike your foot
against a stone.

¹³You will tread upon the lion and the cobra;
you will trample the great lion and the serpent.

The psalmist describes the security of believers with two pictures. Believers are pictured as birds who escape from the trap of the hunter and find shelter under the wings of the mother bird. The hunter and his trap may well represent Satan and his schemes. Believers are also pictured as people trapped in a besieged city who, nevertheless, are delivered from plague and the assaults of the enemy. Together these two pictures represent all the dangers a believer faces in this life. The believer will be preserved from such dangers until he witnesses God's judgment against his enemies.

In verse 9 the psalmist injects a personal touch by restating the faith he shares with the reader. A special source of their assurance is the ministry of the holy angels, whom God uses to watch over and protect his people. Scripture does not state that each believer has one particular angel who watches over him, but the idea of guardian angels who watch over believers is scriptural. Jesus quoted this passage during his temptation as a statement of the way God watches over us in the normal course of our lives. Today when many skeptics debunk the doctrine of angels, it is important that we cling to the comfort that the unseen presence of the angels provides.

Lions and poisonous snakes may represent mortal dangers, but it is striking that elsewhere in Scripture both of these animals are representatives of Satan. If verse 13 is not a direct reference to Satan, it is at least a reminder of the scriptural truth that Satan is the instigator of the threats against the lives of believers. But as God promised already in the Garden of Eden, through the power of Christ, we will trample Satan's head (Genesis 3:15).

The closing verses of the psalm are God's promise of protection. The words marked by half brackets in verse 14 are not in the Hebrew text but were inserted by the translator to indicate the change of speakers. Such unmarked changes of speaker are common in Hebrew poetry. Note the chiastic arrangement, a reversal in the order of words in two otherwise parallel phrases, of verse 14.

## God's promise of deliverance

<sup>14</sup>**"Because he loves me,"** ⌊says the Lord,⌋
    **"I will rescue him;**
    **I will protect him,**
  **for he acknowledges my name.**

<sup>15</sup> **He will call upon me,**
  **and I will answer him;**
  **I will be with him in trouble,**
  **I will deliver him and honor him.**
<sup>16</sup>**With long life will I satisfy him**
  **and show him my salvation."**

These words promise fulfillment of the Seventh Petition, "Deliver us from evil." This is fulfilled when God delivers us from every evil of body and soul and brings us safely into his heavenly kingdom. Although eventually death will overtake every believer except those still living when judgment day dawns, Christ will bring us through death into our eternal home.

# Psalm 92

### *It is good to praise the Lord*

This psalm is connected to the two preceding psalms by its emphasis on safety and prosperity until old age. Its call to praise makes it appropriate for the Sabbath. It shows that the Sabbath of the Old Testament was to be a joyful occasion of public worship, not a burden. True worship brings an increase of joy.

**A psalm. A song. For the Sabbath day.**

*A call to praise*

<sup>1</sup>**It is good to praise the Lord**
**and make music to your name, O Most High,**
<sup>2</sup>**to proclaim your love in the morning**
**and your faithfulness at night,**
<sup>3</sup>**to the music of the ten-stringed lyre**
**and the melody of the harp.**

<sup>4</sup>**For you make me glad by your deeds, O Lord;**
**I sing for joy at the works of your hands.**
<sup>5</sup>**How great are your works, O Lord,**
**how profound your thoughts!**

The opening section of the psalm expresses the joy of praising God in public worship. Throughout the history of the church, music has been one way of expressing this joy. The psalmist also declares the reasons for his joy: the greatness of God's deeds of creation and redemption and the wonderful thoughts revealed in his Word.

The sad end of the wicked, who refuse to acknowledge God, forms a contrast with the joy of believers.

## *The folly and fall of the wicked*

⁶ **The senseless man does not know,**
  **fools do not understand,**
⁷ **that though the wicked spring up like grass**
  **and all evildoers flourish,**
  **they will be forever destroyed.**

⁸ **But you, O Lᴏʀᴅ, are exalted forever.**

⁹ **For surely your enemies, O Lᴏʀᴅ,**
  **surely your enemies will perish;**
  **all evildoers will be scattered.**

This section reviews a theme that we have seen frequently in Psalms. Though the wicked may enjoy brief prosperity, they will fall under the eternal judgment of God. This theme is discussed at length in Psalm 73.

## *The blessing of the righteous*

¹⁰ **You have exalted my horn like that of a wild ox;**
  **fine oils have been poured upon me.**
¹¹ **My eyes have seen the defeat of my adversaries;**
  **my ears have heard the rout of my wicked foes.**

¹² **The righteous will flourish like a palm tree,**
  **they will grow like a cedar of Lebanon;**
¹³ **planted in the house of the Lᴏʀᴅ,**
  **they will flourish in the courts of our God.**
¹⁴ **They will still bear fruit in old age,**
  **they will stay fresh and green,**

¹⁵**proclaiming, "The Lᴏʀᴅ is upright;**
**he is my Rock, and there is no wickedness in him."**

Believers will receive power (a horn) and prosperity (fine oil) from God. Fine oil also indicates the preparation to serve God. Believers will be like a long-lived tree, because they will produce fruits of praise to God both in time and in eternity. They are not immature saplings but sturdy trees, which do not lose their ability to produce fruit, even in old age.

Verse 11 connects Psalm 92 with verse 8 of Psalm 91. Witnessing the final defeat of God's enemies will bring the saints final assurance of the truth of God's promises. When God's enemies are uprooted, his people will endure like a tree planted in his presence. The psalm closes with an emphasis not on our possessions but on God's character.

# Psalms 93–100

Psalms 93 to 100 develop the theme of praise begun in Psalm 92. These psalms revolve around the two themes "The Lord reigns" and "Sing unto the Lord."

# Psalm 93

## *The Lord rules the world*

Psalm 93 proclaims the Lord's unshakeable power over all creation. The repetition of words and phrases throughout the psalm adds to the power of this proclamation.

¹ **The Lᴏʀᴅ reigns,**
**he is robed in majesty;**
**the Lᴏʀᴅ is robed in majesty**
**and is armed with strength.**
**The world is firmly established;**
**it cannot be moved.**

²Your throne was established long ago;
  you are from all eternity.

³ The seas have lifted up, O LORD,
  the seas have lifted up their voice;
  the seas have lifted up their pounding waves.
⁴Mightier than the thunder of the great waters,
  mightier than the breakers of the sea—
  the LORD on high is mighty.

⁵ Your statutes stand firm;
  holiness adorns your house for endless days,
      O LORD.

To the ancient peoples, the power of the sea was terrifying. Even for us today, few things are more awesome than a storm at sea. God's power over the sea is therefore a fitting symbol of his power over all creation. God enclosed the sea in boundaries at creation and again after the flood. When he came in the flesh, he calmed Galilee's storms. This assures us that he rules the world with a majesty that is unchanged since eternity and will continue undiminished even when this world passes away.

The physical world is established and stable only because God's throne is established in heaven. When he withdraws his sustaining power, the world will pass away. But even when the heavens and the earth pass away, God and his Word will not pass away.

# Psalm 94

## *The Lord rules the wicked*

Calls for God's vengeance against his enemies and the enemies of the psalmist are frequent in the psalms, especially in the psalms of David in the first two books of Psalms. For example, Psalms 9, 10, and 13 have themes very similar to that of Psalm 94. A general discussion of such "imprecatory psalms" is found in the introduction to *Psalms 1–72*.

The psalmist begins Psalm 94 with a call for God's avenging justice.

*Introduction*
> ¹O LORD, the God who avenges,
> O God who avenges, shine forth.
> ²Rise up, O Judge of the earth;
> pay back to the proud what they deserve.
> ³How long will the wicked, O LORD,
> how long will the wicked be jubilant?

In God revenge is not evil, since it is not based on whim or an unforgiving spirit. God's revenge is simply the just punishment for sin that flows from God's holy nature. God has provided a payment for sin, but those who scorn that payment will have to answer for their own sins on judgment day. They will pay the penalty their sin deserves, and that penalty is eternal death in hell.

The prayer "How long" is a prayer for God to come in judgment. It has the same content as such New Testament prayers as "Your kingdom come" and "Even so, come, Lord Jesus." Even the saints in heaven pray for God's avenging justice (Revelation 6:10). The next section of the psalm summarizes the deeds of the ungodly, which make their punishment well deserved.

*The deeds of the wicked*
> ⁴They pour out arrogant words;
> all the evildoers are full of boasting.
> ⁵They crush your people, O LORD;
> they oppress your inheritance.

⁶They slay the widow and the alien;
  they murder the fatherless.
⁷They say, "The Lord does not see;
  the God of Jacob pays no heed."

⁸ Take heed, you senseless ones among the people;
  you fools, when will you become wise?

The judgment of the ungodly is not due simply to the fact that they have sinned. We all have sinned often. The problem is that they are indifferent to their sin and defiant toward God's call to repentance. They demonstrate their hatred for God by singling out his people for persecution. They prey especially on the weak and helpless. They are confident that they will get away with their sins.

In spite of this, God calls them to repentance. He invites them to come to true wisdom—the wisdom of God's plan of salvation through Christ. The arrogant accuse God of paying no heed to sin, but the tables are turned when God warns, "It is you who had better take heed of your sins before it is too late."

## *Relief for the righteous*

⁹Does he who implanted the ear not hear?
  Does he who formed the eye not see?
¹⁰Does he who disciplines nations not punish?
  Does he who teaches man lack knowledge?
¹¹The Lord knows the thoughts of man;
  he knows that they are futile.

¹² Blessed is the man you discipline, O Lord,
  the man you teach from your law;
¹³you grant him relief from days of trouble,
  till a pit is dug for the wicked.
¹⁴For the Lord will not reject his people;
  he will never forsake his inheritance.

¹⁵Judgment will again be founded on righteousness,
and all the upright in heart will follow it.

¹⁶Who will rise up for me against the wicked?
Who will take a stand for me against evildoers?
¹⁷Unless the LORD had given me help,
I would soon have dwelt in the silence of death.
¹⁸When I said, "My foot is slipping,"
your love, O LORD, supported me.
¹⁹When anxiety was great within me,
your consolation brought joy to my soul.

²⁰Can a corrupt throne be allied with you—
one that brings on misery by its decrees?
²¹They band together against the righteous
and condemn the innocent to death.
²²But the LORD has become my fortress,
and my God the rock in whom I take refuge.
²³He will repay them for their sins
and destroy them for their wickedness;
the LORD our God will destroy them.

Each paragraph of this section reflects on a different aspect of the relief God brings to his people.

The opening verses are a transition from the deeds of the wicked to the security of God's people. God's knowledge of every human thought rebukes the false security of the wicked and strengthens the confidence of his people. God knows the pride of the arrogant. They will not get away with it! God knows the needs of his people. They will not be forgotten!

The second section explains both why judgment may be delayed for a while and why judgment eventually must come. God may not rescue his people immediately, so that they can be disciplined and strengthened by testing. In this way God trained and strengthened David during the years he was hounded by Saul. But God will bring relief at the right time. Both his love and his justice require that he provide relief for his people.

The third section expresses the psalmist's confidence in question-and-answer form. Who is a help in time of trouble? Who else but the Lord! Now the psalmist is confident, but he formerly fell from this confidence. Like the author of Psalm 73, he almost slipped from faith, but God's love and comfort sustained him. Reflection on God's mercy and goodness put his anxious fears to rest.

The psalmist closes with a final pronouncement of judgment against corrupt, oppressive rulers. Because they have been given a responsibility and a trust, rulers will be judged with special severity when they abuse that trust. God, the holy and merciful ruler, cannot tolerate a ruler who is cruel and corrupt. Corrupt rulers will not be able to make a deal with the heavenly judge, as they often can with earthly judges. God will bring every such ruler to justice. Then the Lord will be a fortress and refuge for his people.

# Psalm 95

## *Worship and warning*

Like the remaining psalms in this group, Psalm 95 sounds a joyful call to worship. However, it also tempers it with a solemn warning against throwing away the opportunity to serve God, as Israel did in the wilderness.

We use the worship section of this psalm in the Matins service as the Venite.

*Worship*
> ¹Come, let us sing for joy to the LORD;
> let us shout aloud to the Rock of our salvation.

²Let us come before him with thanksgiving
 and extol him with music and song.
³For the LORD is the great God,
 the great King above all gods.
⁴In his hand are the depths of the earth,
 and the mountain peaks belong to him.
⁵The sea is his, for he made it,
 and his hands formed the dry land.
⁶Come, let us bow down in worship,
 let us kneel before the LORD our Maker;
⁷for he is our God
 and we are the people of his pasture,
 the flock under his care.

Each of the two invitations to worship in this section is followed by an explanation giving a reason for the invitation. The first reason for praising and thanking God is his work of creation and preservation of the world. These verses echo Psalm 93. The second reason for praising God is his work of redemption and sanctification, by which he made us his people. Because he provides for all our needs of body and soul, let us sing for joy to the Lord.

This psalm reminds us that true worship combines joy (Sing! Shout! Thank! Extol!) with reverence (Bow down! Kneel!).

*Warning*

Today, if you hear his voice,
⁸do not harden your hearts
 as you did at Meribah,
 as you did that day at Massah in the desert,
⁹where your fathers tested and tried me,
 though they had seen what I did.
¹⁰For forty years I was angry with that generation;
 I said, "They are a people whose hearts go astray,
 and they have not known my ways."

**¹¹So I declared on oath in my anger,
"They shall never enter my rest."**

In the Garden of Eden, God gave Adam and Eve peace,
rest, and the opportunity to serve him, but they forfeited
these when they sinned. When God led the Israelites out of
Egypt, he promised them freedom from slavery and rest in a
good land, where they would be free to serve him. But
many of the people threw this opportunity away by their
disobedience and rebellion in the wilderness.

There were two places in the wilderness named
Meribah ("quarreling") and Massah ("testing") because
the Israelites twice argued against God's leadership and
provoked him by complaining about his care for them
(Exodus 17:1-7; Numbers 20:1-13). Because of these provo-
cations and many similar acts of rebellion, God swore that
those who rejected him would never enter rest in the
Promised Land.

Today we have been promised a rest more perfect
and more complete than Israel's rest in the Promised
Land. After Adam and Eve sinned, God promised to send
a Savior to restore the fellowship with God that had been
broken by sin. Throughout the Old Testament era, God's
people kept the Sabbath as a day of rest to remind them
of the perfect rest from sin that the coming Savior would
provide for them. We are experiencing part of that rest
now through the peace with God that we have through
the forgiveness of sins. We will enter the fullness of that
rest when we enter the promised land of heaven.

The "today" of this psalm is this very minute. The "you"
addressed in this psalm is you. In chapters 3 and 4 of the letter to the Hebrews, we are warned not to lose our opportunity for rest as the Israelites did. They heard the promise of
God's rest preached to them, but they did not benefit from it,

because they did not receive it with faith. Today we have the promise of God's eternal rest preached to us. Today, while there still is time, today, before it is too late, let us embrace God's promise of rest. Let us make the enjoyment of that rest our highest goal. Let us make every effort to enter that rest, so that none of us falls short through unbelief.

# Psalms 96–98

## *Joy to the world*

Psalms 96 to 98 are very closely related. They express the joy that the Lord's rule brings to the whole earth. Our Christmas hymn "Joy to the World" is based on the message of these psalms. Since the content of these psalms is so similar, comments on certain points of Psalm 96 will not be repeated in the commentary on Psalms 97 and 98 when the same thoughts reoccur in those psalms.

# Psalm 96

## *The Lord reigns; sing to the Lord a new song*

Psalm 96, together with portions of Psalms 105 and 106, was delivered when David brought the ark of the covenant to Jerusalem (1 Chronicles 16). This psalm is a joyful, majestic call to worship. All creation, including even inanimate nature, is called to worship the Lord.

### *Call to worship*

<sup></sup> ¹**Sing to the LORD a new song;
sing to the LORD, all the earth.
²Sing to the LORD, praise his name;
proclaim his salvation day after day.**

³ **Declare his glory among the nations,**
**his marvelous deeds among all peoples.**

All the peoples of the earth are called to sing to the Lord, because he has provided salvation for the whole world. Christ won peace and forgiveness not only for Israel but for all people. Since Christ died for all the world, God's people are to proclaim the message of salvation to the whole world.

Spreading the message of salvation requires a new song because we are announcing God's new covenant, established by Christ's blood, which was given and shed for us. The "old way" of trying to achieve salvation by works must be cast aside. The heathen must give up their futile, self-invented efforts to find God and sing a new song to the Lord. This song remains ever new because we never outgrow our need for it, nor should we ever grow tired of it. There should be nothing lifeless or stale about our worship.

## *Praise him alone*

⁴ **For great is the LORD and most worthy of praise;**
**he is to be feared above all gods.**
⁵ **For all the gods of the nations are idols,**
**but the LORD made the heavens.**
⁶ **Splendor and majesty are before him;**
**strength and glory are in his sanctuary.**

⁷ **Ascribe to the LORD, O families of nations,**
**ascribe to the LORD glory and strength.**
⁸ **Ascribe to the LORD the glory due his name;**
**bring an offering and come into his courts.**
⁹ **Worship the LORD in the splendor of his holiness;**
**tremble before him, all the earth.**
¹⁰ **Say among the nations, "The LORD reigns."**
**The world is firmly established,**
**it cannot be moved;**
**he will judge the peoples with equity.**

Only the Lord deserves praise. He alone is the Creator of the universe. He alone is the ruler of the universe. He alone is the Savior of the world. He alone is coming to judge the world. All the people of the world should cast aside their useless idols—idols of wood and stone, idols of gold and silver, idols of wealth and power, idols of their own abilities and achievements. They should cast aside their idols and give glory to the Lord alone. The Lord reigns! Let all the people praise him! Let the whole world praise him!

*Let nature praise him*

<sup></sup>
> ¹¹ **Let the heavens rejoice,**
>   **let the earth be glad;**
>   **let the sea resound,**
>   **and all that is in it;**
> ¹² **let the fields be jubilant,**
>   **and everything in them.**
>   **Then all the trees of the forest**
>       **will sing for joy;**
> ¹³ **they will sing before the Lᴏʀᴅ,**
>   **for he comes,**
>   **he comes to judge the earth.**
>   **He will judge the world in righteousness**
>   **and the peoples in his truth.**

Even the created world praises the Lord for his acts of salvation. Nature did not sin, nor is it capable of sinning. But when man sinned, the whole created world came under the curse of sin. Animals suffer and die. Plants suffer from disease and drought. Nature is wracked by storms and earthquakes. Our environment, which was created for our benefit, often battles against us.

When Christ returns and restores peace and harmony to God's creation, the natural world will be free from the effects of sin. The natural world does not need forgiveness of sin, but it does need redemption from the effects of sin. In Romans chapter 8 Paul tells us: "The creation waits in eager expectation for the sons of God to be revealed. For the creation was subjected to frustration, not by its own choice, but by the will of the one who subjected it, in hope that the creation itself will be liberated from its bondage to decay and brought into the glorious freedom of the children of God" (verses 19-21).

This world will not simply be put out of its misery; it will be brought into the glorious freedom of the children of God. When Christ returns, there will be new heavens and a new earth, which will serve as our eternal home (Revelation 21,22). Our eternal home will apparently have elements of nature, like those in the first Eden but more glorious. Since all creation will be restored to unblemished service of God and man, all creation is described as joining in the joyful song of the redeemed.

The repetition and crisp wording of this psalm create a feeling of joy and excitement as we anticipate Christ's return. Although Scripture solemnly warns us to be prepared for the Last Day, joy and eagerness, not fear and reluctance, should be the predominant feelings we have as we await that day. When that day comes, we should lift up our heads with joy as we see our redemption drawing near. Then we will join the whole creation in singing a new song to the Lord throughout all eternity.

# Psalm 97

### *The Lord reigns; cast aside your idols*

Psalm 97 develops one aspect of Psalm 96 more fully, namely, the futility of idols. Verse 7, in the middle of the psalm, is the key to the psalm.

## Introduction

¹ **The LORD reigns, let the earth be glad;
let the distant shores rejoice.**

## God will judge

² **Clouds and thick darkness surround him;
righteousness and justice are the foundation
of his throne.**
³ **Fire goes before him
and consumes his foes on every side.**
⁴ **His lightning lights up the world;
the earth sees and trembles.**
⁵ **The mountains melt like wax before the LORD,
before the Lord of all the earth.**
⁶ **The heavens proclaim his righteousness,
and all the peoples see his glory.**

Clouds, darkness, lightning, and fire all represent the awesome power of God, which will be displayed on judgment day. God's wrath against sin, which is partially hidden now, will be fully displayed then. The world and the universe that surrounds it will be burned up with fire. Christ will appear in the clouds and shine from one end of the sky to the other. Unbelievers will hide in terror. Yet for God's people, the awesome events of that day will be a cause for joy.

Righteousness and justice are the basis of God's judgment. He will come to repay torment to the tormentors of his people. He will bring relief to those who suffered because of their loyalty to him. He will bring salvation to all who have trusted in Christ for forgiveness.

## Admonition against idolatry

⁷ **All who worship images are put to shame,
those who boast in idols—
worship him, all you gods!**

Since judgment is surely coming, those who worship idols should repent before it is too late. If they do not, their confidence will be turned to shame. Their idols will not help them when God's judgment comes. In fact, the idols themselves will be subjected to God's judgment. The idols will be revealed as nothing, and Satan and his angels, who hide behind the mask of the idols, will bow to Christ in submission (1 Corinthians 8:4; 10:20; Philippians 2:10). The "gods" (verse 7) who bow to Christ on judgment day may include the good angels, who serve him with joy, and the evil angels, who submit to him with dismay.

*His people's response*

> ⁸ **Zion hears and rejoices**
> **and the villages of Judah are glad**
> **because of your judgments, O Lᴏʀᴅ.**
> ⁹ **For you, O Lᴏʀᴅ, are the Most High**
> **over all the earth;**
> **you are exalted far above all gods.**
> ¹⁰ **Let those who love the Lᴏʀᴅ hate evil,**
> **for he guards the lives of his faithful ones**
> **and delivers them from the hand of the wicked.**
> ¹¹ **Light is shed upon the righteous**
> **and joy on the upright in heart.**
>
> ¹² **Rejoice in the Lᴏʀᴅ, you who are righteous,**
> **and praise his holy name.**

The joy God's saints find in his judgments has been expressed in the preceding psalms of this group. The special feature of this repetition of that theme is found in verse 10: "Let those who love the Lᴏʀᴅ hate evil." Those who love the Lord must battle God's enemies. This battle may be painful and costly, but we are assured of God's protecting power. Those who love good must shun and oppose evil.

Because of the toleration and open-mindedness of our time, it is all too easy for Christians to be silent or even comfortable in the presence of evil. But God will tolerate no evil, and we must not either. While we as sinners must humbly recognize sin in ourselves, this must not lead us to minimize the evil of sin in ourselves or others. The solution to sin and evil is not toleration or whitewashing but forgiveness from Christ. Only then can we rejoice in Christ's coming.

# Psalm 98

## *The Lord reigns; sing to the Lord a new song*

Psalm 98 is an echo of Psalms 93 and 96. Many of the comments on Psalm 96 also apply to Psalm 98.

**A psalm.**

*Invitation*

**¹Sing to the LORD a new song,**
**for he has done marvelous things;**
**his right hand and his holy arm**
**have worked salvation for him.**

*Let his people sing*

**²The LORD has made his salvation known**
**and revealed his righteousness to the nations.**
**³He has remembered his love and his faithfulness**
**to the house of Israel;**
**all the ends of the earth have seen**
**the salvation of our God.**

*Let all people sing*

> [4]**Shout for joy to the L**ORD**, all the earth,**
> **burst into jubilant song with music;**
> [5]**make music to the L**ORD **with the harp,**
> **with the harp and the sound of singing,**
> [6]**with trumpets and the blast of the ram's horn—**
> **shout for joy before the L**ORD**, the King.**

*Let the whole earth sing*

> [7]**Let the sea resound, and everything in it,**
> **the world, and all who live in it.**
> [8]**Let the rivers clap their hands,**
> **let the mountains sing together for joy;**
> [9]**let them sing before the L**ORD**,**
> **for he comes to judge the earth.**
> **He will judge the world in righteousness**
> **and the peoples with equity.**

Unlike its predecessors, Psalm 98 is almost pure praise. Idols and enemies have receded into the background. All we see is the Lord's throne. The Lord is surrounded by ever-widening circles of praise. As he had promised, the Lord first made his salvation known to Israel. Israel was to tell the nations so that they too could join in the song. Finally, all creation joins the song.

Taken together, Psalms 96, 97, and 98 express both the delight and the doom God's judgment will bring. This theme is developed extensively in the second half of Isaiah and in the many New Testament passages that deal with Christ's return.

# Psalm 99

### *He rules in Israel*

Psalm 99 is closely related to the three psalms that precede it. Although the judgment of Israel's enemies is still mentioned here, the focus has shifted to God's gracious dealings with his people.

## Warning to the nations

> ¹ **The LORD reigns,**
> **let the nations tremble;**
> **he sits enthroned between the cherubim,**
> **let the earth shake.**
> ² **Great is the LORD in Zion;**
> **he is exalted over all the nations.**
> ³ **Let them praise your great and awesome name—**
> **he is holy.**

The holiness of God is mentioned three times in this psalm. God dwells in unapproachable majesty. The holiness and majesty of God terrify sinners. Even the cherubim, the angels who are merely servants who wait around God's throne, are so awesome that they strike terror into man. However, this holy God has made it possible for sinners to be restored to his presence. God gave a foreshadowing of his eternal dwelling with his people when his glory appeared in his temple in Jerusalem. There the golden cherubim, which hovered over the ark of the covenant, symbolized the Lord's presence. Though his people were undeserving, he was present with his saving power.

## Assurance to Israel

> ⁴ **The King is mighty, he loves justice—**
> **you have established equity;**
> **in Jacob you have done what is just and right.**
>
> ⁵ **Exalt the LORD our God**
> **and worship at his footstool;**
> **he is holy.**

⁶ **Moses and Aaron were among his priests,**
   **Samuel was among those who called on his name;**
   **they called on the LORD and he answered them.**
⁷ **He spoke to them from the pillar of cloud;**
   **they kept his statutes**
   **and the decrees he gave them.**
⁸ **O LORD our God, you answered them;**
   **you were to Israel a forgiving God,**
   **though you punished their misdeeds.**
⁹ **Exalt the LORD our God**
   **and worship at his holy mountain,**
   **for the LORD our God is holy.**

The holiness of God is a comfort to his people who are repentant. They are twice invited to come and worship the holy God. They can come with confidence because of God's attribute of justice; he will be faithful to his promise to provide forgiveness and salvation. They can come with confidence because of his past performance; again and again he forgave the Israelites' sins when they returned to him in repentance.

Through intercessors like Moses and Samuel, Israel sought forgiveness and found it. God often imposed disciplinary chastisements on his wayward people, but he did not cast them aside. He restored them to the joy of serving at his holy mountain. This psalm, which speaks so majestically of the lofty holiness of God, ends on a note of intimacy: he is holy, but he is our God.

# Psalm 100

## *He rules his people*

This little gem completes the group of psalms describing the Lord's rule. It contains two invitations to worship, each

Temple musician

of which is followed by a supporting reason for worship. The pure joy of this psalm has made it very popular in Christian worship.

**A psalm. For giving thanks.**

¹ Shout for joy to the LORD, all the earth.
² Worship the LORD with gladness;
come before him with joyful songs.

³ Know that the LORD is God.
It is he who made us, and we are his;
we are his people, the sheep of his pasture.

⁴ Enter his gates with thanksgiving
and his courts with praise;
give thanks to him and praise his name.

⁵ For the LORD is good and his love endures forever;
his faithfulness continues through all generations.

True worship is based on knowing who God is and what he has done. We can sing a joyful song to the Lord because he has made us and redeemed us. God made mankind to serve him, but the whole human race went astray. Nevertheless, God sent Jesus, the Good Shepherd, to lead us back to him. Jesus returned us to God's flock. Although we were locked out of God's presence by our sin, we can now enter the gates of his sanctuary.

We are confident that we will never be excluded again, because Jesus promised that no one will take his sheep out of his hands. Since God is good, loving, and faithful, we know that this promise will stand firm forever. Joy and gladness, thanksgiving and praise flow naturally from hearts and lips that know the Lord's goodness. Let us come before him with joyful songs.

# Psalms 101–110

Psalms 101 to 110 are quite loosely connected. The group begins and ends with a description of the Davidic king. In general it deals with the experiences that the king and his subjects share. However, the interconnections within this group are much less clear than those in the preceding group of psalms.

# Psalm 101

### *The good ruler*

In Psalm 101 we have a portrait of the ideal king. He is devoted to serving God. He carries out the duty of a ruler to support the good and oppose the evil.

**Of David. A psalm.**

¹**I will sing of your love and justice;**
**to you, O Lord, I will sing praise.**
²**I will be careful to lead a blameless life—**
**when will you come to me?**
**I will walk in my house with blameless heart.**

In this opening section, David declares his devotion to serving the Lord. One way he will serve him is by singing his praises. This David did especially through the psalms he wrote. David will also serve the Lord with a godly life. He recognizes that personal piety is essential for those who wish to be spiritual leaders to others. David expresses his eagerness for fellowship with God by the question "When will you come to me?" (verse 2).

In the second section of the psalm, David promises that he will not tolerate evil men in his kingdom.

³I will set before my eyes no vile thing.
  The deeds of faithless men I hate;
  they will not cling to me.
⁴Men of perverse heart shall be far from me;
  I will have nothing to do with evil.
⁵Whoever slanders his neighbor in secret,
      him will I put to silence;
  whoever has haughty eyes and a proud heart,
      him will I not endure.
⁶My eyes will be on the faithful in the land,
  that they may dwell with me;
  he whose walk is blameless will minister to me.
⁷No one who practices deceit will dwell in my house;
  no one who speaks falsely will stand
      in my presence.
⁸Every morning I will put to silence
      all the wicked in the land;
  I will cut off every evildoer
      from the city of the LORD.

The most basic duties God has given to rulers are to oppose and punish evil and to protect and encourage good. Rulers who condone or tolerate evil or who hinder good conduct are a disgrace to the position God gave them. David pledges that his government will oppose evil and that he will not allow the wicked to serve in his government. He wants godly men as his associates and as his subjects. He will not promote officials who serve only to feed their own pride or those who advance themselves by slandering and betraying others. David will do everything in his power to drive evil out of the land.

This is one of only two psalms in Book 4 that are explicitly ascribed to David by the heading. We may understand this psalm as an expression of David's intentions as a king. David was an exceptional ruler, but nevertheless, he fell far short of the ideal expressed in this psalm.

Godliness begins at home. There is a tragic irony in verse 2 because it was in his house that David's troubles began and continued. David's failure to reach the standard he had set was due especially to his adultery with Bathsheba and his murder of her husband, Uriah. This failure in his own family life severely handicapped him in his efforts to oppose wickedness among his sons. As a king he was not able to control the violence of his ruthless army commander Joab. In spite of good intentions, David fell short of the ideal portrait of a king outlined in this psalm.

Although this psalm is not cited as messianic in the New Testament, we recognize that Christ was the only Davidic king who fully lived up to the characteristics of the ideal king outlined in this psalm. He was completely devoted to serving his Father. He led a sinless life. He supports everything that is good and opposes every evil. When he returns as judge, he will remove every evil person and every hypocrite from God's holy city. When he comes, God's people will have the righteous king they have longed for.

# Psalm 102

## *The afflicted ruler*

The heading of Psalm 102 is very unusual, with its general description of an unnamed author. There is nothing in it to link it to a specific event in the life of David. The biblical story that best fits the circumstances of this psalm is the prolonging of Hezekiah's life for 15 years after God had told him that his life was about to end. In Isaiah chapter 38 there is a psalm that Hezekiah wrote in response to that situation. It is very similar to Psalm 102.

Although this psalm has traditionally been classified as one of the penitential psalms, that is not its main focus. It contrasts the shortness of human life with the eternity of God.

**A prayer of an afflicted man. When he is faint and pours out
his lament before the L**ORD**.**

## *Opening plea*

¹ **Hear my prayer, O L**ORD**;**
**let my cry for help come to you.**
² **Do not hide your face from me**
**when I am in distress.**
**Turn your ear to me;**
**when I call, answer me quickly.**

In this short opening plea, the psalmist asks for the
Lord's help in his distress. In the following section, he
describes that distress more fully.

## *The shortness of his days*

³ **For my days vanish like smoke;**
**my bones burn like glowing embers.**
⁴ **My heart is blighted and withered like grass;**
**I forget to eat my food.**
⁵ **Because of my loud groaning**
**I am reduced to skin and bones.**
⁶ **I am like a desert owl,**
**like an owl among the ruins.**
⁷ **I lie awake;**
**I have become like a bird alone on a roof.**
⁸ **All day long my enemies taunt me;**
**those who rail against me use my name as a curse.**
⁹ **For I eat ashes as my food**
**and mingle my drink with tears**
¹⁰ **because of your great wrath,**
**for you have taken me up and thrown me aside.**
¹¹ **My days are like the evening shadow;**
**I wither away like grass.**

The psalmist's distress is caused by an awareness of the impending end of his own life, by God's wrath against sin, and by the reproaches of his enemies. He describes the shortness of his own life in a number of striking poetic pictures. His life is like withering grass, vanishing smoke, an evening shadow. He is as lonely as an owl in the desert or a solitary bird on a rooftop. He has lost his appetite, so his food tastes like ashes. All of these feelings correspond quite closely with the emotions expressed in Hezekiah's psalm in Isaiah chapter 38.

The shortness of the psalmist's life contrasts sharply with the endlessness of God's reign.

## God's endless years

<sup></sup>12 But you, O LORD, sit enthroned forever;
   your renown endures through all generations.
13 You will arise and have compassion on Zion,
   for it is time to show favor to her;
   the appointed time has come.
14 For her stones are dear to your servants;
   her very dust moves them to pity.

15 The nations will fear the name of the LORD,
   all the kings of the earth will revere your glory.
16 For the LORD will rebuild Zion
   and appear in his glory.
17 He will respond to the prayer of the destitute;
   he will not despise their plea.
18 Let this be written for a future generation,
   that a people not yet created may praise the LORD:
19 "The LORD looked down from his sanctuary on high,
   from heaven he viewed the earth,
20 to hear the groans of the prisoners
   and release those condemned to death."

²¹ **So the name of the L**ORD **will be declared in Zion**
  **and his praise in Jerusalem**
²² **when the peoples and the kingdoms assemble**
    **to worship the L**ORD**.**

The words "But you, O LORD" are the dramatic turning point from distress to triumph. The Lord's eternal power will solve the psalmist's dilemma. The sudden concern for Zion suggests that the psalm was written at a time when Jerusalem and its people were in danger. This also corresponds well with the time of Hezekiah, when the threat of capture by the Assyrians was hanging over Jerusalem.

In any case, the psalmist's prayer is not just for himself but for the city and people of Jerusalem. He is confident that God will preserve the city so that its people will be free to continue serving the Lord. If this prayer was written by Hezekiah or some other king, he is praying that he be allowed to live so that he can lead the battle for Jerusalem. However, he is confident that God will be there to grant the victory regardless of whether the king departs or remains.

People will continue to praise the Lord into the distant future for this great victory.

## The plea repeated

²³ **In the course of my life he broke my strength;**
  **he cut short my days.**
²⁴ **So I said: "Do not take me away, O my God,**
    **in the midst of my days;**

The psalmist repeats his plea for rescue from a premature death. The plea is repeated here to provide a sharp contrast between the shortness of the psalmist's life and the eternity of God described in the following verses.

Compare this plea with that of Hezekiah in Isaiah 38:10: "I said, 'In the prime of my life must I go through the gates of death and be robbed of the rest of my years?'"

## *The eternal king*

> your years go on through all generations.
> <sup>25</sup> In the beginning you laid the foundations
> of the earth,
> and the heavens are the work of your hands.
> <sup>26</sup> They will perish, but you remain;
> they will all wear out like a garment.
> Like clothing you will change them
> and they will be discarded.
> <sup>27</sup> But you remain the same,
> and your years will never end.
>
> <sup>28</sup> The children of your servants will live
> in your presence;
> their descendants will be established before you."

This majestic description of the eternity of God reminds us of Psalm 90. In the context of the psalm, this section appears to be the completion of the king's plea to God. However, in Hebrews 1:10-12 these words are quoted as a description of the eternity of Christ.

In the Septuagint, the Greek translation of the Old Testament, verse 23 is translated in such a way as to make verses 25 to 28 the words of God to the sufferer, rather than the words of the suffering king to God. According to this rendering, it is the suffering king who will have endless years. According to this understanding, the suffering king is Christ, and the whole psalm is messianic. Even if the sufferer of the psalm is first Hezekiah or some other king of Israel who was cut off in the midst of his days, the psalmist could still serve as a type of Christ, who was cut off in the midst of his days yet had eternal years.

However, if we stay with the rendering of the standard Hebrew text, which seems to be the most natural reading, verses 25 to 28 are words of the psalmist addressed to God. They may nevertheless be applied to Christ, since he is God. Although it is tempting to follow the Septuagint reading, which suggests that the psalm is directly messianic or at least typically messianic, it seems best to remain with the Hebrew reading, which makes the psalm a messianic psalm by application to the Son of a statement that applies to the triune God. Verses 25 to 27 would not refer exclusively to Christ but to the triune God, including God the Son. In either case, it is the eternity of the triune God that is the solution to the psalmist's suffering.

# Psalm 103

## *Praise the Lord; he forgives all your sins*

Psalms 103 and 104 form a pair. They are united by the theme "Praise the Lord, O my soul." Psalm 103 praises the Lord for his work of redemption. Psalm 104 praises him for creation.

Psalm 103 is one of only two psalms in Book 4 that are attributed to David by the heading. Psalm 103 is one of the most beautiful psalms of comfort. It is especially appropriate during sickness or hospitalization.

**Of David.**

*Introduction*

    ¹**Praise the LORD, O my soul;**
    **all my inmost being, praise his holy name.**

*Praise for personal blessings*

> ² **Praise the LORD, O my soul,**
>   **and forget not all his benefits—**
> ³ **who forgives all your sins**
>   **and heals all your diseases,**
> ⁴ **who redeems your life from the pit**
>   **and crowns you with love and compassion,**
> ⁵ **who satisfies your desires with good things**
>   **so that your youth is renewed like the eagle's.**

David thanks God for the blessings he has experienced in his life. These blessings were both physical and spiritual. David had been lavishly blessed with power and possessions. He had been satisfied with good things. He had soared like an eagle to fame and fortune. However, he became estranged from God by his grievous sins of adultery and murder.

We do not know whether Psalm 103 was written after these sins, but if it was, it is a follow-up to such penitential psalms as Psalms 32 and 51. The joining together of sin and sickness connects Psalm 103 with such penitential psalms as Psalms 6 and 38. In these psalms the sickness he suffered reminded David of his guilt. Whether the sickness and forgiveness mentioned in these psalms followed David's adultery and murder or some other less notorious sins in his life makes no difference. The principle of associating sin and sickness would be the same in either case.

In one sense every sickness is a result of sin. If sin had not entered the world, there would be no sickness. Every sickness reminds us that we are sinners living in a sinful world. Sometimes a specific sickness is the result of a specific sin. Sicknesses transmitted or caused by drug abuse or sexual immorality are examples of such diseases.

God may send sickness to punish unbelievers, as he did when he sent plagues against Egypt. Sicknesses may also be sent to chasten or correct believers (1 Corinthians 11:29,30). However, we cannot draw the conclusion that every sickness is the result of a specific sin. God may have some other reason for allowing sicknesses to enter our lives, such as strengthening our faith or displaying his glory. Examples of such sicknesses are those of Job or of the man born blind (John 9).

We can say with certainty that no sickness of a Christian is punishment for sin in the strict sense. Christ has already been punished for our sins, so no further punishment is necessary. Our debt has been paid, and it does not have to be paid again. This truth will be made clear in the next part of this psalm, as David turns from his personal blessings to the blessings of the nation.

## Praise for blessing on the nation

> <sup>6</sup> The Lord works righteousness and justice
>     for all the oppressed.
> <sup>7</sup> He made known his ways to Moses,
>   his deeds to the people of Israel:
> <sup>8</sup> The Lord is compassionate and gracious,
>   slow to anger, abounding in love.
> <sup>9</sup> He will not always accuse,
>   nor will he harbor his anger forever;
> <sup>10</sup> he does not treat us as our sins deserve
>   or repay us according to our iniquities.

In many respects the history of Israel was like David's personal history. Like David, Israel had received undeserved mercy and forgiveness. The people had often gone astray during the wilderness years, but God forgave them and maintained his covenant with them. Verse 8 is a quotation of God's declaration to Moses after Israel's sin of worshiping the golden calf (Exodus 34:6). True to his nature and true to his promise, the Lord did not treat the Israelites as their sins deserved. He did chasten them and correct them. He did remove the unbelievers from the nation. But he did not destroy the people or cast the nation aside. He forgave their sins and restored them to fellowship with him.

The Lord has not dealt with us as our sins deserve. He has forgiven our sins for Christ's sake. Since he has given his own Son to die for us, we can feel absolutely sure of his love. Even sickness and death cannot separate us from his love. This assurance is a great comfort when sickness tempts us to doubt God's love. The second half of Romans chapter 8 develops this theme more fully.

## God's mercy illustrated

> <sup>11</sup> **For as high as the heavens are above the earth,**
>   **so great is his love for those who fear him;**
> <sup>12</sup> **as far as the east is from the west,**
>   **so far has he removed our transgressions from us.**
> <sup>13</sup> **As a father has compassion on his children,**
>   **so the LORD has compassion on those who fear him;**
> <sup>14</sup> **for he knows how we are formed,**
>   **he remembers that we are dust.**

God's mercy and forgiveness are immeasurable. Who can measure the distance of the east from the west? Who can measure the height of the sky? God's love will never come to an end. God's supply of forgiveness will never run out. When God removes sin, he removes it completely. He is not like people who forgive but don't forget. When God forgives sin, he does not bring it up again. It is important to remember this when we are haunted by sins of the past. Since God has forgiven them, they are gone for good. Our consciences should no longer accuse us when God has declared us forgiven.

A second illustration compares God's manner of dealing with us to that of a loving father. Good parents love their children and hope for the best from them, but they do not expect or demand more than their children are capable of performing at a given age and level of ability. God knows the limitations imposed on us by our present physical and spiritual weaknesses. He does not demand from us more than we can perform. What we are incapable of doing, Christ has done for us.

We can learn something about the character of God from observing a good parent, but the opposite is even more true. Earthly fathers are not always very good representations of what God is like, but God is always a good model of what an earthly father should be like. Parents can find no better example to imitate.

*Man's short life and God's eternal mercy*

> <sup>15</sup> **As for man, his days are like grass,**
>     **he flourishes like a flower of the field;**
> <sup>16</sup> **the wind blows over it and it is gone,**
>     **and its place remembers it no more.**
> <sup>17</sup> **But from everlasting to everlasting**
>     **the LORD's love is with those who fear him,**
>     **and his righteousness with their**
>         **children's children—**
> <sup>18</sup> **with those who keep his covenant**
>     **and remember to obey his precepts.**
> <sup>19</sup> **The LORD has established his throne in heaven,**
>     **and his kingdom rules over all.**

Psalm 103 provides an answer to Psalm 90, the psalm of Moses that began Book 4. Psalm 90 focuses on the shortness of human life as a judgment against sin. Psalm 103 focuses on God's eternal love as the power that overcomes the shortness of human life.

Human life is very fleeting. In comparison to God's eternity or the age of the earth, it is as short as the life of a flower. Some flowers, like the daylily, flourish for only a day. We know how quickly a flower withers when it is cut or broken off. In the same way a human life can be cut short in a day. But this fact does not discourage God's children.

God's children are those who believe his gospel covenant. They show themselves to be his children when they obey his commandments. God's love remains for his children from generation to generation. It will still be with us after we have died, when our bodies rest in the grave and our souls are kept in heaven. God's love will uphold our children and grandchildren when we are no longer present to support them. It will continue to bless us all when we are rejoined in eternity. God's kingdom is established, and we will live in it forever.

## Invitation to praise

> <sup>20</sup>Praise the LORD, you his angels,
>   you mighty ones who do his bidding,
>   who obey his word.
> <sup>21</sup>Praise the LORD, all his heavenly hosts,
>   you his servants who do his will.
> <sup>22</sup>Praise the LORD, all his works
>     everywhere in his dominion.
>   Praise the LORD, O my soul.

The psalm concludes with an invitation to all creatures to praise the Lord. We join David in saying, "Bless the LORD, O my soul."

# Psalm 104

## *Praise the Lord; he creates wonders*

Psalm 104 celebrates the wonders of God's creation, particularly as it provides a home for man and God's other creatures. This psalm is arranged according to the days of creation in Genesis chapter 1. However, it directs our attention not so much to the creation as to the Creator. Genesis chapters 1 and 2 are an account of creation; Psalm 104 is a celebration of the wisdom and love of the Creator.

## *Introduction*

> ¹ Praise the LORD, O my soul.
> O LORD my God, you are very great;
> you are clothed with splendor and majesty.

## *Day 1*

> ² He wraps himself in light as with a garment;

## *Day 2*

> he stretches out the heavens like a tent
> ³ and lays the beams of his upper chambers
>          on their waters.
> He makes the clouds his chariot
> and rides on the wings of the wind.
> ⁴ He makes winds his messengers,
> flames of fire his servants.

This introduction provides a summary of the glory due to God as the Creator. The creation itself testifies to his glory (Psalm 19).

On the first day of creation, before any light sources existed, God made light simply by speaking. God is the source of all light. Because light is the first of God's creations and makes the rest of God's creation visible, it is often used as a symbol of the life and joy God gives.

Even today scientists do not fully understand this most basic element of God's creation. They resort to various theories of waves and particles to account for the behavior of light, but light remains a mystery known only to God. Explaining even the first step of God's creation eludes man's grasp. How appropriate, then, to call light the glorious garment in which God clothes himself.

On the second day, God distinguished the earth from its atmosphere and from the space that surrounds it. The heavens are called the floor of God's dwelling, since he dwells above and beyond this created universe. Because God is the master of the elements and they do his bidding, he is pictured as riding on clouds and winds.

Verse 4 could also be translated, "He makes his messengers winds, his servants flames of fire." According to this translation, verse 4 would refer to the speed and splendor of the angels. Since this translation is grammatically possible and since it is the translation accepted in Hebrews 1:7, it is preferable to the rendering of the NIV. The NIV translation, which refers to winds and flames as God's messengers, creates a better synonymous parallel with verse 3, which refers to winds and clouds, but it also creates a redundancy, since the text then mentions winds twice. It would not be unusual to have verse 3 mention elements of the physical heavens and verse 4 jump to the inhabitants of the heaven of spirits, since these two forces are often set side by side in Scripture. For example, the heavenly hosts may be either the stars or the angels.

## Day 3

⁵ He set the earth on its foundations;
 it can never be moved.
⁶ You covered it with the deep as with a garment;
 the waters stood above the mountains.
⁷ But at your rebuke the waters fled,
 at the sound of your thunder they took to flight;
⁸ they flowed over the mountains,
 they went down into the valleys,
 to the place you assigned for them.
⁹ You set a boundary they cannot cross;
 never again will they cover the earth.
¹⁰ He makes springs pour water into the ravines;
 it flows between the mountains.
¹¹ They give water to all the beasts of the field;
 the wild donkeys quench their thirst.
¹² The birds of the air nest by the waters;
 they sing among the branches.
¹³ He waters the mountains from his upper chambers;
 the earth is satisfied by the fruit of his work.
¹⁴ He makes grass grow for the cattle,
 and plants for man to cultivate—
 bringing forth food from the earth:
¹⁵ wine that gladdens the heart of man,
 oil to make his face shine,
 and bread that sustains his heart.
¹⁶ The trees of the LORD are well watered,
 the cedars of Lebanon that he planted.
¹⁷ There the birds make their nests;
 the stork has its home in the pine trees.
¹⁸ The high mountains belong to the wild goats;
 the crags are a refuge for the coneys.

On day 3 God separated water from dry land, and he created plants. The psalmist elaborates on this aspect of creation because the control of the sea is one of the most awesome displays of God's power and because water and the plants that it sustains are two essential elements for providing food for animals and human beings. Water and plants are discussed in relation to the service they provide for human beings and animals.

Wine, olive oil, and bread were the three basic foods of ancient Israelites. Incidentally, this reference shows that wine is a gift of God if it is used, not abused.

The coney is an animal that looks somewhat like a badger or prairie dog.

*Day 4*

> ¹⁹ The moon marks off the seasons,
>   and the sun knows when to go down.
> ²⁰ You bring darkness, it becomes night,
>   and all the beasts of the forest prowl.
> ²¹ The lions roar for their prey
>   and seek their food from God.
> ²² The sun rises, and they steal away;
>   they return and lie down in their dens.
> ²³ Then man goes out to his work,
>   to his labor until evening.

On day 4 God created the sun, moon, and stars. The Genesis account stresses their role in marking times and seasons for mankind. The psalmist also observes how these heavenly bodies signal the beginning and ending of periods of activity for the inhabitants of the earth.

*Days 5 and 6*

> ²⁴ How many are your works, O LORD!
>   In wisdom you made them all;
>   the earth is full of your creatures.

²⁵ There is the sea, vast and spacious,
   teeming with creatures beyond number—
   living things both large and small.
²⁶ There the ships go to and fro,
   and the leviathan, which you formed
       to frolic there.

²⁷ These all look to you to give them their food
       at the proper time.
²⁸ When you give it to them,
   they gather it up;
   when you open your hand,
   they are satisfied with good things.
²⁹ When you hide your face,
   they are terrified;
   when you take away their breath,
   they die and return to the dust.
³⁰ When you send your Spirit,
   they are created,
   and you renew the face of the earth.

On days 5 and 6, God created animate life, including man and woman. These animate creatures are dealt with briefly here since they have already been introduced in the sections on water and the heavenly bodies.

Leviathan is the name for a great sea monster. Here it may refer to the whale. Whether leviathan here represents the whale or a legendary sea monster, the point is the same. To God the hugest, most awe-inspiring creatures are like playful little puppies.

The psalmist emphasizes the way in which God provides food and life to his creatures. God gives food as the normal way of sustaining life, but we are not to forget that life comes from God. God breathed the breath of life into Adam, and he returned Adam to the dust again. God gives life to each new generation, and he calls each generation back to dust again. God is the lifegiver, God is the life-sustainer—this is the key theme of Psalm 104.

*Closing benediction and prayer*

> [31] May the glory of the L‍ORD endure forever;
>   may the L‍ORD rejoice in his works—
> [32] he who looks at the earth, and it trembles,
>   who touches the mountains, and they smoke.
> [33] I will sing to the L‍ORD all my life;
>   I will sing praise to my God as long as I live.
> [34] May my meditation be pleasing to him,
>   as I rejoice in the L‍ORD.
>
> [35] But may sinners vanish from the earth
>   and the wicked be no more.
>
> Praise the L‍ORD, O my soul.
> Praise the L‍ORD.

The psalmist closes with the prayer that God will continue to preserve his creation and to rule it with justice. He promises to praise God for this work of creation and preservation. Using our memory and mind to reflect on God's work of redemption and creation should stir up our emotions and our will to praise the Lord. Motivating such praise is the goal of Psalms 103 and 104.

# Psalms 105 and 106

Psalms 105 and 106, which conclude Book 4, are closely related in both theme and origin. Both of them are "historical review" psalms, similar to such psalms as Psalm 78. They are also similar to the prayer in Nehemiah chapter 9. These two psalms complement each other as positive and negative presentations of the same story. Psalm 105 emphasizes God's faithfulness to his covenant. Psalm 106 focuses on Israel's unfaithfulness and disobedience, which resulted in judgment.

These two psalms are also related in origin. The first 15 verses of Psalm 105 are the opening verses of the psalm David presented when the ark of the covenant was brought to Jerusalem (1 Chronicles 16). The introduction and conclusion to Psalm 106 form the conclusion of David's psalm for the ark. The middle of the ark psalm appears in the psalter as Psalm 96. We do not know whether David composed the psalm for bringing up the ark by selecting portions from Psalms 96, 105, and 106, which he had composed previously, or whether Psalms 105 and 106 were written later as a fuller commentary on the opening verses of the ark psalm. The latter seems more likely.

Many commentators believe that these two psalms were written as a commentary on David's ark psalm many years after David's time by Ezra or some contemporary of his, but there is nothing in the historical review that goes past the time of David. The reference to captivity in foreign lands in Psalm 106:47 can be harmonized with Davidic authorship by the fact that Moses had prophesied such captivity in Deuteronomy four hundred years before David's time. Although these psalms may have been written long before the exile, they were certainly a special comfort after the return from exile, when Israel was a small remnant, struggling to reestablish itself in the land.

Since most of the verses of these psalms are simply restatements of historical accounts, we will not comment on them extensively, other than to point out their location in the historical books.

# Psalm 105

## *God remembers his covenant*

### *Introduction*

> ¹ **Give thanks to the LORD,**
>  **call on his name;**
>  **make known among the nations what he has done.**
> ² **Sing to him, sing praise to him;**
>  **tell of all his wonderful acts.**
> ³ **Glory in his holy name;**
>  **let the hearts of those who seek the LORD rejoice.**
> ⁴ **Look to the LORD and his strength;**
>  **seek his face always.**
> ⁵ **Remember the wonders he has done,**
>  **his miracles, and the judgments he pronounced,**
> ⁶ **O descendants of Abraham his servant,**
>  **O sons of Jacob, his chosen ones.**
> ⁷ **He is the LORD our God;**
>  **his judgments are in all the earth.**

The introduction admonishes Israel to look to the Lord for help. It encourages such faith by reminding the people of the Lord's great deeds in the past. "I am the LORD your God" is the declaration God had made to Israel when he gave the Law at Mount Sinai. By mentioning Abraham and Jacob, God's "chosen ones" with whom he had established the covenant, the psalm points ahead to God's faithfulness to his covenant, which is emphasized in the rest of the psalm.

Most of the rest of the psalm is a review of the Lord's past faithfulness to the covenant, arranged in historical order.

### *The covenant*

> ⁸ **He remembers his covenant forever,**
>  **the word he commanded, for a thousand generations,**
> ⁹ **the covenant he made with Abraham,**
>  **the oath he swore to Isaac.**

<sup>10</sup> He confirmed it to Jacob as a decree,
   to Israel as an everlasting covenant:
<sup>11</sup> "To you I will give the land of Canaan
   as the portion you will inherit."

The promise to Abraham, Isaac, and Jacob had three main points: the promised seed, the great nation, and the land. In the days of David and Ezra, the great nation had already been formed, and the promised seed was still to come. Since the point at stake in those times was possession of the land, so the nation could be preserved and the seed could come, the land is naturally the point of emphasis in these psalms.

## Faithful in Canaan

<sup>12</sup> When they were but few in number,
   few indeed, and strangers in it,
<sup>13</sup> they wandered from nation to nation,
   from one kingdom to another.
<sup>14</sup> He allowed no one to oppress them;
   for their sake he rebuked kings:
<sup>15</sup> "Do not touch my anointed ones;
   do my prophets no harm."

<sup>16</sup> He called down famine on the land
   and destroyed all their supplies of food;
<sup>17</sup> and he sent a man before them—
   Joseph, sold as a slave.
<sup>18</sup> They bruised his feet with shackles,
   his neck was put in irons,
<sup>19</sup> till what he foretold came to pass,
   till the word of the LORD proved him true.
<sup>20</sup> The king sent and released him,
   the ruler of peoples set him free.

<sup>21</sup>He made him master of his household,
ruler over all he possessed,
<sup>22</sup>to instruct his princes as he pleased
and teach his elders wisdom.

This section describes how God preserved Israel in the land of Canaan. The main reference of verse 15 is to Genesis 20:7. When Abraham and Isaac got into trouble by their own lies and deception (Genesis 12,20,26), God protected them from the kings of Egypt and Philistia. He protected Jacob from Laban and from Esau (Genesis 28–33). He protected Jacob when Jacob's sons stirred up the hostility of the land by their slaughter of the Shechemites (Genesis 34). Finally, he saved them from famine and from being absorbed by the Canaanites by sending Joseph to Egypt to prepare a place for them (Genesis 37).

## Faithful in Egypt

<sup>23</sup>Then Israel entered Egypt;
Jacob lived as an alien in the land of Ham.
<sup>24</sup>The LORD made his people very fruitful;
he made them too numerous for their foes,
<sup>25</sup>whose hearts he turned to hate his people,
to conspire against his servants.
<sup>26</sup>He sent Moses his servant,
and Aaron, whom he had chosen.
<sup>27</sup>They performed his miraculous signs among them,
his wonders in the land of Ham.
<sup>28</sup>He sent darkness and made the land dark—
for had they not rebelled against his words?
<sup>29</sup>He turned their waters into blood,
causing their fish to die.
<sup>30</sup>Their land teemed with frogs,
which went up into the bedrooms of their rulers.
<sup>31</sup>He spoke, and there came swarms of flies,
and gnats throughout their country.

³²He turned their rain into hail,
  with lightning throughout their land;
³³he struck down their vines and fig trees
  and shattered the trees of their country.
³⁴He spoke, and the locusts came,
  grasshoppers without number;
³⁵they ate up every green thing in their land,
  ate up the produce of their soil.
³⁶Then he struck down all the firstborn
      in their land,
  the firstfruits of all their manhood.
³⁷He brought out Israel, laden with silver and gold,
  and from among their tribes no one faltered.
³⁸Egypt was glad when they left,
  because dread of Israel had fallen on them.

In Egypt the Lord blessed the Israelites doubly. First he fulfilled the promise that they would be a great nation. Then he freed them from Pharaoh's tyranny by sending the plagues on Egypt (Exodus 1–13).

## Faithful in the wilderness

³⁹He spread out a cloud as a covering,
  and a fire to give light at night.
⁴⁰They asked, and he brought them quail
  and satisfied them with the bread of heaven.
⁴¹He opened the rock, and water gushed out;
  like a river it flowed in the desert.

The psalmist very briefly summarizes God's protection and provision for Israel during the wilderness years. Exodus chapters 14 to 17 describe the beginning of this care. It continued throughout the wanderings of the wilderness years, which are described in Numbers and Deuteronomy.

*Conclusion*

⁴²**For he remembered his holy promise**
**given to his servant Abraham.**

⁴³ **He brought out his people with rejoicing,**
**his chosen ones with shouts of joy;**
⁴⁴**he gave them the lands of the nations,**
**and they fell heir to what others had toiled for—**
⁴⁵**that they might keep his precepts**
**and observe his laws.**
**Praise the LORD.**

Verse 42 is the key to the psalm. God's remembrance of his covenant is more than a calling to mind. It is taking decisive action for the benefit of his people. God's faithfulness was not due to Israel's worthiness but to his own faithfulness to the promise he had made to the patriarchs. God announced this fact when he called Moses to lead Israel out of Egypt (Exodus 2:24; 3:6; 4:2-5).

The Israelites needed to be reminded of this truth throughout their history. They also needed to be reminded of the purpose for which God had redeemed them from Egypt and given them freedom in their own land. He had not freed them so that they could indulge in idolatry. He had freed them so that they could obey his laws and serve him.

This psalm is more than ancient history. Through faith we belong to Abraham's family (Galatians 3,4). These chapters are the beginnings of church history. The same principles set forth in this psalm apply to Christians today. God has redeemed us from sin and continues to forgive our sins, not because we are worthy but because of his faithfulness to the gospel covenant that he established through Christ's death and resurrection. The Lord has forgiven us freely, not so we can indulge in sin but so we will serve him gladly.

The plagues

# Psalm 106

## *Israel forgot*

Psalm 106 covers the same historical ground as Psalm 105, but it looks at the dark side of the picture. Israel repeatedly forgot God's goodness and rebelled against his commands. Nevertheless, this dark psalm is not without light. In spite of Israel's sin, God's grace abounded, and he remained faithful to his covenant.

### *Introduction*

Praise the LORD.
Give thanks to the LORD,
for he is good;
his love endures forever.

² Who can proclaim the mighty acts of the LORD
or fully declare his praise?
³ Blessed are they who maintain justice,
who constantly do what is right.

⁴ Remember me, O LORD, when you show favor
to your people,
come to my aid when you save them,
⁵ that I may enjoy the prosperity
of your chosen ones,
that I may share in the joy of your nation
and join your inheritance in giving praise.

The introduction calls on God's people to be thankful for his goodness, not ungrateful like Israel. Who can convincingly proclaim God's Word? Only those whose thankfulness is visible in their devotion to obeying God's Word. Israel's testimony was hampered by its disobedience, which is cataloged in the rest of the psalm.

The psalmist combines his personal faith with a concern for sharing that faith within the fellowship of God's people. Christian worship should avoid both the loss of personal involvement that comes from being swallowed up in the crowd and the loss of fellowship with the group, which comes from retreating into isolation.

The concern for sharing in the blessings of God's people expressed in verses 4 and 5 is expressed frequently in the book of Nehemiah. The emphasis on the past and present sins of the nation, which is presented in the following verses of the psalm, is also an emphasis of the book of Nehemiah.

## Israel forgot

**⁶We have sinned, even as our fathers did;**
**we have done wrong and acted wickedly.**

## Rebellion in Egypt

**⁷When our fathers were in Egypt,**
**they gave no thought to your miracles;**
**they did not remember your many kindnesses,**
**and they rebelled by the sea, the Red Sea.**

## God's grace

**⁸Yet he saved them for his name's sake,**
**to make his mighty power known.**
**⁹He rebuked the Red Sea, and it dried up;**
**he led them through the depths**
**as through a desert.**
**¹⁰He saved them from the hand of the foe;**
**from the hand of the enemy he redeemed them.**
**¹¹The waters covered their adversaries;**
**not one of them survived.**
**¹²Then they believed his promises**
**and sang his praise.**

## *Rebellion in the wilderness*

¹³ But they soon forgot what he had done
  and did not wait for his counsel.
¹⁴ In the desert they gave in to their craving;
  in the wasteland they put God to the test.
¹⁵ So he gave them what they asked for,
  but sent a wasting disease upon them.
¹⁶ In the camp they grew envious of Moses
          and of Aaron,
  who was consecrated to the LORD.
¹⁷ The earth opened up and swallowed Dathan;
  it buried the company of Abiram.
¹⁸ Fire blazed among their followers;
  a flame consumed the wicked.
¹⁹ At Horeb they made a calf
  and worshiped an idol cast from metal.
²⁰ They exchanged their Glory for an image of a bull,
          which eats grass.
²¹ They forgot the God who saved them,
  who had done great things in Egypt,
²² miracles in the land of Ham
  and awesome deeds by the Red Sea.

## *God's grace*

²³ So he said he would destroy them—
  had not Moses, his chosen one,
  stood in the breach before him
  to keep his wrath from destroying them.

## *More rebellion in the wilderness*

²⁴ Then they despised the pleasant land;
  they did not believe his promise.
²⁵ They grumbled in their tents
  and did not obey the LORD.

²⁶ So he swore to them with uplifted hand
 that he would make them fall in the desert,
²⁷ make their descendants fall among the nations
 and scatter them throughout the lands.
²⁸ They yoked themselves to the Baal of Peor
 and ate sacrifices offered to lifeless gods;
²⁹ they provoked the LORD to anger
  by their wicked deeds,
 and a plague broke out among them.
³⁰ But Phinehas stood up and intervened,
 and the plague was checked.
³¹ This was credited to him as righteousness
 for endless generations to come.
³² By the waters of Meribah they angered the LORD,
 and trouble came to Moses because of them;
³³ for they rebelled against the Spirit of God,
 and rash words came from Moses' lips.

This section catalogs some of the many rebellions in Egypt and the wilderness, but it does not list them in chronological order. The principal rebellions listed are the grumbling at the Red Sea (Exodus 14:11), the demand for meat (Numbers 11), the rebellion of Korah, Dathan, and Abiram against Moses (Numbers 16), the golden calf at Mount Sinai (Exodus 32), the refusal to go into the land after the return of the spies (Numbers 14), the idolatry and sexual immorality at Baal Peor (Numbers 25), and the demand for water at Meribah (Exodus 17; Numbers 20).

God gave two responses to Israel's apostasy. He sent chastening judgments. Even Moses was unable to enter the Land of Promise, because he faltered at the rock of Meribah and usurped God's honor for himself. Yet throughout all these judgments, God's grace remained. Faithful to his promise, he heard the prayers of Moses on behalf of the people. Exodus chapters 32 to 34 provide a prime example of such intercession.

Other people who remained loyal to the Lord were the Levites, who put an end to the idolatry at Sinai, and Phineas, the high priest-to-be, who stopped the idolatry at Baal Peor. Their faithfulness was rewarded with the promise that they would be able to serve the Lord. Nevertheless, it was not such limited human faithfulness that saved Israel. It was the unlimited grace of God.

## Rebellion in the land

³⁴ They did not destroy the peoples
   as the Lord had commanded them,
³⁵ but they mingled with the nations
   and adopted their customs.
³⁶ They worshiped their idols,
   which became a snare to them.
³⁷ They sacrificed their sons
         and their daughters to demons.
³⁸ They shed innocent blood,
   the blood of their sons and daughters,
   whom they sacrificed to the idols of Canaan,
   and the land was desecrated by their blood.
³⁹ They defiled themselves by what they did;
   by their deeds they prostituted themselves.

⁴⁰ Therefore the Lord was angry with his people
   and abhorred his inheritance.
⁴¹ He handed them over to the nations,
   and their foes ruled over them.
⁴² Their enemies oppressed them
   and subjected them to their power.
⁴³ Many times he delivered them,
   but they were bent on rebellion
   and they wasted away in their sin.

## God's grace

> <sup>44</sup> **But he took note of their distress**
> **when he heard their cry;**
> <sup>45</sup> **for their sake he remembered his covenant**
> **and out of his great love he relented.**
> <sup>46</sup> **He caused them to be pitied**
> **by all who held them captive.**

Israel's history of rebellion continued in the land. The people not only tolerated the idolatrous Canaanites; they adopted their ways. One terrible feature of the Canaanite worship was human sacrifice, especially of one's own children. Israel adopted this practice to such a degree that the judge Jephthah apparently could not see the evil of sacrificing his daughter to the Lord (Judges 11). Such sacrifice became common also during the monarchy under such corrupt kings as Manasseh.

The cycles of idolatry, captivity, short-lived repentance, and relief that are described in these verses of the psalm are based on the principal theme of the book of Judges, but such cycles continued during the monarchy as well.

## Prayer

> <sup>47</sup> **Save us, O LORD our God,**
> **and gather us from the nations,**
> **that we may give thanks to your holy name**
> **and glory in your praise.**

This prayer for restoration so that the nation could serve the Lord was appropriate during the days of David, after the dark days of the judges and Saul, and during the days of Ezra and Nehemiah, after the exile in Babylon.

142

*Doxology*

> ⁴⁸ **Praise be to the LORD, the God of Israel,**
> **from everlasting to everlasting.**
> **Let all the people say, "Amen!"**
> **Praise the LORD.**

This doxology concludes both Psalm 106 and Book 4 of Psalms. In 1 Chronicles 16:36 the second half of the verse is given as a statement: "All the people said 'Amen' and 'Praise the LORD.'"

Like the preceding psalm, Psalm 106 was written not just to review history but to teach us a lesson. Israel's bad example and the sad results it produced should warn us against repeating such behavior. Let us be on guard, lest we take God's grace for granted and squander the blessings it has provided.

# BOOK FIVE

## *Psalms 107–150*

In general, Book 5 continues the style and format of Book 4. However, the clear grouping of psalms by category is more pronounced in Book 5. Examples of such groupings are Davidic collections (Psalms 108–110, 138–145), the Passover hallel (Psalms 113–118), songs of ascents (Psalms 120–134), and hallelujah psalms (Psalms 146–150).

# Psalm 107

## *He redeemed them from trouble*

Although Psalm 107 begins a new book, it continues the theme of Psalms 105 and 106. Like them it calls on the redeemed to thank God for his gracious deliverance. However, Psalm 107 is much different in style. Notice, for example, the refrains that conclude each section.

Another major difference is that Psalm 107 is less historical than the preceding psalms. It may allude to the exile and other historical events indirectly, but instead of clearly citing specific historical events as its examples of deliverance, it uses four general situations: wandering in the desert, release from prison, forgiveness after rebellion, and danger on the sea. Perhaps these general situations are intended to represent Israel's captivity in Babylon or spiritual dangers.

### Introduction

> ¹**Give thanks to the L**ORD**, for he is good;**
> **his love endures forever.**
> ²**Let the redeemed of the L**ORD **say this—**
> **those he redeemed from the hand of the foe,**
> ³**those he gathered from the lands,**
> **from east and west,**
> **from north and south.**

The introduction seems to connect the psalm with the captivity in Babylon. It thanks the Lord for regathering his people from the nations. In this way it is an answer to the prayer for gathering that concludes Psalm 106.

## First crisis

> ⁴ Some wandered in desert wastelands,
>   finding no way to a city where they could settle.
> ⁵ They were hungry and thirsty,
>   and their lives ebbed away.
>
> ⁶ Then they cried out to the LORD in their trouble,
>   and he delivered them from their distress.
> ⁷ He led them by a straight way
>   to a city where they could settle.
>
> ⁸ Let them give thanks to the LORD
>   for his unfailing love
>   and his wonderful deeds for men,
> ⁹ for he satisfies the thirsty
>   and fills the hungry with good things.

The first crisis is similar to Israel's wandering in the wilderness, but it is more generalized and universal in application.

## Second crisis

> ¹⁰ Some sat in darkness and the deepest gloom,
>   prisoners suffering in iron chains,
> ¹¹ for they had rebelled against the words of God
>   and despised the counsel of the Most High.
> ¹² So he subjected them to bitter labor;
>   they stumbled, and there was no one to help.
>
> ¹³ Then they cried out to the LORD in their trouble,
>   and he saved them from their distress.
> ¹⁴ He brought them out of darkness
>       and the deepest gloom
>   and broke away their chains.
>
> ¹⁵ Let them give thanks to the LORD
>   for his unfailing love
>   and his wonderful deeds for men,

<sup></sup>¹⁶ **for he breaks down gates of bronze
and cuts through bars of iron.**

The second crisis corresponds in a general way to
Israel's experiences in Egypt and Babylon, but again it
is generalized.

## *Third crisis*

¹⁷ **Some became fools through their rebellious ways
and suffered affliction
because of their iniquities.**
¹⁸ **They loathed all food
and drew near the gates of death.**

¹⁹ **Then they cried out to the LORD in their trouble,
and he saved them from their distress.**
²⁰ **He sent forth his word and healed them;
he rescued them from the grave.**

²¹ **Let them give thanks to the LORD
for his unfailing love
and his wonderful deeds for men.**
²² **Let them sacrifice thank offerings
and tell of his works with songs of joy.**

The third crisis could apply to almost any period of
Israel's history. It occurred over and over again during the
time of the judges and kings.

## *Fourth crisis*

²³ **Others went out on the sea in ships;
they were merchants on the mighty waters.**
²⁴ **They saw the works of the LORD,
his wonderful deeds in the deep.**

²⁵ For he spoke and stirred up a tempest
  that lifted high the waves.
²⁶ They mounted up to the heavens
  and went down to the depths;
  in their peril their courage melted away.
²⁷ They reeled and staggered like drunken men;
  they were at their wits' end.

²⁸ Then they cried out to the LORD in their trouble,
  and he brought them out of their distress.
²⁹ He stilled the storm to a whisper;
  the waves of the sea were hushed.
³⁰ They were glad when it grew calm,
  and he guided them to their desired haven.

³¹ Let them give thanks to the LORD
  for his unfailing love
  and his wonderful deeds for men.
³² Let them exalt him in the assembly of the people
  and praise him in the council of the elders.

Seafaring was not common among the Israelites. The story of Jonah is the only Old Testament account that compares with this psalm. Nevertheless, Israel was fascinated with the sea as the most awesome part of God's creation. In a storm at sea, the best efforts of ancient mariners counted for little. They were helpless before the power of wind and wave. Therefore God's control over the sea was considered the outstanding display of his power. The disciples were especially impressed when Jesus stilled the storm.

## Curses and blessings

³³ He turned rivers into a desert,
  flowing springs into thirsty ground,
³⁴ and fruitful land into a salt waste,
  because of the wickedness of those who lived there.

³⁵ He turned the desert into pools of water
   and the parched ground into flowing springs;
³⁶ there he brought the hungry to live,
   and they founded a city where they could settle.
³⁷ They sowed fields and planted vineyards
   that yielded a fruitful harvest;
³⁸ he blessed them,
   and their numbers greatly increased,
   and he did not let their herds diminish.
³⁹ Then their numbers decreased,
   and they were humbled
         by oppression, calamity and sorrow;
⁴⁰ he who pours contempt on nobles
         made them wander in a trackless waste.
⁴¹ But he lifted the needy out of their affliction
   and increased their families like flocks.
⁴² The upright see and rejoice,
   but all the wicked shut their mouths.

This section reiterates the principles concerning blessings and curses that are set forth at the end of Leviticus and Deuteronomy: obeying God leads to blessing; disobeying God results in a curse. The territory around Sodom and Gomorrah is a prime example of good land that became a wasteland because of its people's sins. This good land, coveted by Lot, is today a barren waste.

The rest of this section corresponds in a general way with Israel's experience in the Promised Land, but the psalmist is more interested in general principles than in historical specifics. The curse expressed in this section received its first fulfillment in the curse on the ground in Genesis chapter 3. The blessing will receive its complete fulfillment only in the new heavens and the new earth.

## Application

> [43] **Whoever is wise,**
> **let him heed these things**
> **and consider the great love of the LORD.**

Because the principles in this psalm are general, their application is universal. All who wish to be wise should apply the principles of this psalm to their own lives. They should take warning from the judgments that fall upon the disobedient. They should be strengthened by the love of God displayed in his blessings upon those who remember his covenant.

The lostness, hunger, confusion, and imprisonment described in this psalm are all used as pictures of man's natural spiritual condition elsewhere in Scripture. The helplessness of sailors in a hurricane is also an apt picture of our natural spiritual condition. It is very likely that these pictures are intended to direct our attention not only to physical dangers but also to our spiritual needs. In the same way, the "city where they could settle" (verse 36) directs our attention beyond Jerusalem and other cities on earth to the city above, which is the home of us all.

# Psalms 108–110

Psalms 108 to 110 are the first grouping of Davidic psalms in Book 5. If Psalm 107, the transitional psalm to Book 5, and the hallelujah psalms, which end Book 5, are excluded, Book 5 begins and ends with Davidic psalms.

# Psalm 108

## *My heart is steadfast*

Psalm 108 is a composite psalm formed by combining the conclusions of Psalms 57 and 60. Psalm 57 is about God's protection of David during his flight from Saul. Psalm 60 thanks God for David's victory over the Arameans of Syria. See Volume 1 for further comments on those psalms.

As it is rearranged here, this psalm has become a praise for God's past acts of deliverance, a prayer for such deliverance in the future, and a statement of confidence in God's help. It is more positive than the psalms from which it was taken. It dwells less on distress than they do, with only a hint of distress remaining in verse 11. It apparently is intended to serve as a more general prayer for deliverance than the two psalms from which it is derived. (See map on page 232.)

**A song. A psalm of David.**

*Praise*

¹ My heart is steadfast, O God;
I will sing and make music with all my soul.
² Awake, harp and lyre! I will awaken the dawn.
³ I will praise you, O Lord, among the nations;
I will sing of you among the peoples.
⁴ For great is your love, higher than the heavens;
your faithfulness reaches to the skies.
⁵ Be exalted, O God, above the heavens,
and let your glory be over all the earth.

*Prayer*

⁶ Save us and help us with your right hand,
that those you love may be delivered.

*Promise and performance*

⁷ God has spoken from his sanctuary:
"In triumph I will parcel out Shechem
and measure off the Valley of Succoth.
⁸ Gilead is mine, Manasseh is mine;
Ephraim is my helmet, Judah my scepter.

⁹**Moab is my washbasin,**
  **upon Edom I toss my sandal;**
  **over Philistia I shout in triumph."**

¹⁰ **Who will bring me to the fortified city?**
  **Who will lead me to Edom?**

¹¹ **Is it not you, O God, you who have rejected us**
  **and no longer go out with our armies?**
¹² **Give us aid against the enemy,**
  **for the help of man is worthless.**
¹³ **With God we will gain the victory,**
  **and he will trample down our enemies.**

Like Psalms 105 to 107, this psalm extols the Lord's faithfulness in helping the Israelites retain the Promised Land in spite of the attacks of their enemies and in spite of their own sins. Though the Lord chastened the Israelites for their sins, he did not abandon them. He delivered them because of his covenant. He helped them conquer all the areas of the land he had promised to them, and he helped them defeat the enemies who surrounded them. If he did this, he would not forsake them in their present distress. With him they would gain the victory.

# Psalm 109

### *Deceitful men have opened their mouths*

Psalm 109 is one of several psalms that contain curses upon the psalmist's enemies. Others are Psalms 55, 56, 58, and 69. The curses contained in these psalms are often shocking to modern readers, but such prayers are in accordance with God's curse against sin. Such prayers are spoken by the Messiah in Psalm 69 and even by the saints in heaven in

Revelation 6:10. For a more detailed statement concerning the general principles pertaining to the interpretation of such "imprecatory psalms," consult the Introduction to the Psalms contained in Volume 1 of this commentary.

**For the director of music. Of David. A psalm.**

## *The problem and the prayer*

¹**O God, whom I praise, do not remain silent,**
²**for wicked and deceitful men have opened**
   **their mouths against me;**
 **they have spoken against me with lying tongues.**
³**With words of hatred they surround me;**
 **they attack me without cause.**
⁴**In return for my friendship they accuse me,**
 **but I am a man of prayer.**
⁵**They repay me evil for good,**
 **and hatred for my friendship.**

In the opening section of this psalm, David states his problem. People who should be his supporters have betrayed him and are speaking lies against him. They are repaying him evil for good. These words probably apply to Ahithophel and others who betrayed David at the time of Absalom's revolt. David speaks against such traitors in Psalms 41 and 55. David also was slandered during the time of his flight from Saul. Psalm 7 addresses this problem.

David does not take matters into his own hands or seek to avenge himself. His solution to slander is to entrust the matter to God. David is a man of prayer.

## *The curse*

⁶**Appoint an evil man to oppose him;**
 **let an accuser stand at his right hand.**

⁷ When he is tried, let him be found guilty,
  and may his prayers condemn him.
⁸ May his days be few;
  may another take his place of leadership.
⁹ May his children be fatherless
  and his wife a widow.
¹⁰ May his children be wandering beggars;
  may they be driven from their ruined homes.
¹¹ May a creditor seize all he has;
  may strangers plunder the fruits of his labor.
¹² May no one extend kindness to him
  or take pity on his fatherless children.
¹³ May his descendants be cut off,
  their names blotted out from the next generation.
¹⁴ May the iniquity of his father be remembered
        before the Lord;
  may the sin of his mother never be blotted out.
¹⁵ May their sins always remain before the Lord,
  that he may cut off the memory of them
        from the earth.

¹⁶ For he never thought of doing a kindness,
  but hounded to death the poor and the needy
        and the brokenhearted.
¹⁷ He loved to pronounce a curse—
  may it come on him;
  he found no pleasure in blessing—
  may it be far from him.
¹⁸ He wore cursing as his garment;
  it entered into his body like water,
  into his bones like oil.
¹⁹ May it be like a cloak wrapped about him,
  like a belt tied forever around him.

²⁰ May this be the Lord's payment to my accusers,
  to those who speak evil of me.

David's call for punishment on his enemy contains a number of harsh curses: may his sins not be forgiven, may he lose his position, may his family share his fate. Harsh as they are, these curses rest on biblical principles. The enemy cannot retain his position because he is using it to harm others. To pray for him to continue in his position would be to pray for evil to prosper. The enemy's sins cannot be forgiven because he is not repentant. He loves to curse. He wraps himself in deceit like a garment. To pray for his sins to be overlooked would be to pray for God to violate his law. Such a prayer a Christian cannot pray.

The references to the liar's family are the most troubling part of the prayer. It is a principle of biblical justice that children should not be punished for the sins of their parents or vice versa (Ezekiel 18). It is also true that God is "a jealous God, punishing the children for the sins of the fathers to the third and fourth generation of those who hate" him (Exodus 20:5). Those who continue in the sinful ways of their parents or ancestors will share in their condemnation.

Families often share in and support the sins of individual family members. This was perhaps more obvious in the ancient Near East, where multigenerational families lived and worked together. Ancient and modern inhabitants of the Near East have much more feeling of group solidarity and shared responsibility and much less feeling of individualism than modern Westerners. This may explain in part the involvement of the enemy's family in his sin. The families of Haman (Esther 5:14; 9:13) and Achan (Joshua 7:24) are two biblical examples of such involvement.

This psalm is apparently an application of the principle from the Ten Commandments that is quoted above. We do not know enough about the circumstances to say much more.

In verse 6 the Hebrew word for *accuser* is *satan*. This and *evil one* are both used as titles of the chief of the evil angels, so it is possible that verse 6 refers to Satan, as the NIV footnote suggests. If so, the liar who opposes David is to be delivered to the kingdom of the master liar, whom he has served.

The closing verses provide a justification for this prayer. It should be done to him as he loved to do to others. This agrees both with the Old Testament principle of justice, "eye for eye" (Exodus 21:24), and with the principle expressed by Jesus' statement "With the measure you use, it will be measured to you" (Luke 6:38).

This prayer is put in its proper perspective by Peter's quotation from it in Acts 1:20. Peter says that the Holy Spirit spoke these words through David concerning Judas Iscariot. The friend who betrayed David was a type of Judas, Jesus' betrayer. In spite of Jesus' loving warnings, Judas persisted in his course, destroyed himself, and was damned. The horrible truth is that all who remain impenitent will be damned. That curse of God makes all the curses of this psalm pale by comparison.

## Prayer for help

> [21] But you, O Sovereign LORD, deal well with me
> for your name's sake;
> out of the goodness of your love, deliver me.
> [22] For I am poor and needy,
> and my heart is wounded within me.
> [23] I fade away like an evening shadow;
> I am shaken off like a locust.
> [24] My knees give way from fasting;
> my body is thin and gaunt.
> [25] I am an object of scorn to my accusers;
> when they see me, they shake their heads.

<sup>26</sup> Help me, O Lᴏʀᴅ my God;
   save me in accordance with your love.
<sup>27</sup> Let them know that it is your hand,
   that you, O Lᴏʀᴅ, have done it.
<sup>28</sup> They may curse, but you will bless;
   when they attack they will be put to shame,
   but your servant will rejoice.
<sup>29</sup> My accusers will be clothed with disgrace
   and wrapped in shame as in a cloak.

In this section David's prayer takes a more positive turn. He bases his plea on God's goodness, love, and mercy. His prayer is that God's name will be hallowed. He states the desperation of his situation with a number of striking poetic comparisons but expresses confidence in God's help.

The statement "They may curse, but you will bless" reminds us of God's promise to Abraham, "I will bless those who bless you, and whoever curses you I will curse" (Genesis 12:3) and of God's frustration of Balaam's attempts to curse Israel (Numbers 23,24). No one can curse God's friends; no one can bless his enemies.

## Closing praise

<sup>30</sup> With my mouth I will greatly extol the Lᴏʀᴅ;
   in the great throng I will praise him.
<sup>31</sup> For he stands at the right hand of the needy one,
   to save his life from those who condemn him.

David closes this prayer with a brief word of praise for God's justice. He delivers this praise in the midst of God's people. He proclaims the Lord's concern for his oppressed people as a general principle, applicable to David, to us, and to all believers.

This psalm spares nothing in its portrayal of the seriousness of sin. It sets forth in graphic terms the terrible consequences of sin. It expresses the full sternness of the law of God. It reminds us and all who read it of the urgency of repentance.

# Psalm 110

### *The Lord says to my Lord*

Psalm 110 is one of the most important messianic psalms. It is quoted or alluded to very often in the New Testament. It consists of two oracles of God the Father concerning his Son, the Messiah.

**Of David. A psalm.**

*First oracle*

¹ **The LORD says to my Lord:**
**"Sit at my right hand**
**until I make your enemies a footstool**
   **for your feet."**

² **The LORD will extend your mighty scepter from Zion;**
**you will rule in the midst of your enemies.**
³ **Your troops will be willing on your day of battle.**
**Arrayed in holy majesty,**
**from the womb of the dawn**
**you will receive the dew of your youth.**

Verse 1 was quoted by Jesus as a proof of his deity (Matthew 22:44). David, the speaker of verse 1, says, "The Lord Yahweh says to my lord and master, 'Sit at my right hand.'" If David, the greatest king of Israel, calls the Messiah his Lord, then the Messiah must be more than David's descendant; he must be true God as well.

It is noteworthy that the whole point of Christ's argument depends on his acceptance of David's authorship of this psalm, a point denied by many critics. Peter made a very similar argument based on Davidic authorship in his Pentecost sermon (Acts 2:29-35).

In biblical times the right hand was the position of power and authority. The term *at the right hand of God* is used frequently in the New Testament to describe Jesus' exaltation after he suffered and died for us. Since his resurrection and ascension, Jesus has exercised all power in heaven and in earth. He rules the whole universe for the benefit of his people.

To use one's enemies as a footstool refers to the ancient custom in which a conqueror placed his foot on his vanquished foes as a display of his triumph. This prophecy will be fulfilled on judgment day, when Christ will complete his conquest of all our enemies, including death, and when Satan and all who have opposed Christ must submit to his rule. The fulfillment of this passage is described in more detail in 1 Corinthians 15:20-28.

Verses 2 and 3 may be understood either as David's comments in response to God's oracle or as the continuation of God's oracle. The punctuation of the NIV suggests the first interpretation, but the second seems preferable. In biblical style it would not be unusual for God to refer to himself in the third person, as "the Lord." The meaning is the same in either case.

Verse 2 describes Christ's universal rule, which includes his powerful rule over his enemies, who submit unwillingly. Verse 3 describes his gracious rule over those who come to him in faith. They gladly join him in the battle against evil. The last part of verse 3 is difficult to translate. It may describe the ageless beauty and majesty of the eternal Christ, who remains as fresh as the dew every morning, or it may describe the freshness of his followers, who receive their strength from him. The first interpretation seems preferable.

## Second oracle

> [4] The LORD has sworn and will not change his mind:
> "You are a priest forever,
>      in the order of Melchizedek."
>
> [5] The Lord is at your right hand;
>
> he will crush kings on the day of his wrath.
> [6] He will judge the nations,
> heaping up the dead
> and crushing the rulers of the whole earth.
> [7] He will drink from a brook beside the way;
> therefore he will lift up his head.

The solemnity and certainty of the second oracle is emphasized by the fact that it is an oath. The Lord's second oracle brings a surprising piece of information. The Messiah, David's son, will not only be a king; he will also be a priest. This is surprising because in the Old Testament the kingship and priesthood were strictly separated. The kings came from David's family of the tribe of Judah. The priests came from Aaron's family of the tribe of Levi. Christ's extraordinary combination of offices indicates that he will be no ordinary priest. He will be a priest in the order of Melchizedek.

Hebrews chapters 4 to 10 explain in considerable detail what it means that Christ is a priest in the order of Melchizedek. Hebrews chapter 7 is the key chapter of this comparison. Melchizedek is a mysterious figure who appears in Genesis chapter 14. He was king of Jerusalem and a priest of the true God. We know nothing about where he came from or about his parents. We know only that he was both a king and a priest and that he became a priest by God's appointment. We know of no predecessors or successors of his. He was unique. He therefore serves as a suitable type of Christ.

Like Melchizedek, Christ received his priesthood by special appointment of God. He was not from the right tribe or family to be a priest. Like Melchizedek, Christ was in a class by himself. God had to send Christ as a unique priest like Melchizedek because all the sacrifices offered by the Old Testament high priests could never on the basis of their own worth free a single sinner from guilt. They offered forgiveness only because they pointed ahead to a greater, more perfect sacrifice. That sacrifice was offered by Christ, the Great High Priest.

The second oracle also raises a question of punctuation and division. At what point does the subject shift from the Father to the Son? It seems most likely that this occurs in the middle of verse 5, as the previous paragraphing indicates. According to this interpretation, the first line of verse 5 is either a continuation of the Father's oracle or a response of David to the Father's oracle. The first interpretation seems more probable.

According to this interpretation, the remainder of the psalm is a description of Christ's power to judge. It is striking that after introducing Christ's priestly office, the psalm so quickly reverts to his power as king and judge. This picture of Christ coming as conqueror reminds us of the way he is portrayed in Revelation chapter 19. After crushing his enemies, he pauses to be refreshed and to enjoy his victory with his troops.

Psalm 110 is one of the most meaningful of the messianic psalms, since it describes Christ as the complete Savior whom we need. He had the love and humility to offer himself as the perfect sacrifice for sin. He has the power to defeat our enemies and to rule as king on our behalf. Let us gladly join his army and be willing troops in the battle against sin and evil.

Christ on his throne of judgment

# Psalms 111 and 112

These two psalms are single-line acrostics. Each line begins with a successive letter of the Hebrew alphabet. These psalms also complement each other in content. Psalm 111 is about God's works and God's Word. It is a good introduction to a whole group of psalms on this theme, which ends with Psalm 119. Psalm 112 describes the upright man who responds to God's works and God's Word.

# Psalm 111

### *God's works and God's Word*

*Opening praise*

> ¹ **Praise the LORD.**
>
> **I will extol the LORD with all my heart**
> **in the council of the upright and in the assembly.**

*God's works*

> ² **Great are the works of the LORD;**
> **they are pondered by all who delight in them.**
> ³ **Glorious and majestic are his deeds,**
> **and his righteousness endures forever.**
> ⁴ **He has caused his wonders to be remembered;**
> **the LORD is gracious and compassionate.**
> ⁵ **He provides food for those who fear him;**
> **he remembers his covenant forever.**
> ⁶ **He has shown his people the power of his works,**
> **giving them the lands of other nations.**
> ⁷ **The works of his hands are faithful and just;**

*God's Word*

> all his precepts are trustworthy.
> <sup>8</sup>They are steadfast for ever and ever,
> done in faithfulness and uprightness.
> <sup>9</sup>He provided redemption for his people;
> he ordained his covenant forever—
> holy and awesome is his name.
> <sup>10</sup>The fear of the LORD is the beginning of wisdom;
> all who follow his precepts
> have good understanding.

*Concluding praise*

> To him belongs eternal praise.

The psalm begins and ends with praise for God's works and his Word. The main body of the psalm is made up of two sections, the first emphasizing God's works, the second emphasizing his Word. These two themes cannot be sharply separated. For example, God's covenant with Israel is mentioned in both sections. God made a covenant promise, and he carried out that promise in Israel's history. What God says in his Word is always put into action. What God does is based on what he has said in his Word.

God's works include works of creation, works of preservation, and works of redemption. As their Creator the Lord provides his people with food. As their Redeemer he brought them out of Egypt into the land he had promised in his covenant with Abraham.

God wanted Israel to remember and ponder these works. The book of Deuteronomy stresses the theme "Do Not Forget." This psalm serves the same purpose. We too are to remember and ponder God's works for us. The three articles of the Apostles' Creed and Luther's explanations of them are designed to help us do this very thing. We remember and ponder God's threefold work of creation, redemption, and sanctification. Praise the Lord for his glorious works!

God's Word tells us what he has done, and it also tells us how we should respond to his deeds. We should believe his promises. They are dependable and will all be fulfilled. We should strive to live according to his commandments. They tell us what is pleasing to God and what is best for our lives. The fear of the Lord, which is awe and respect for all that he has revealed and done, is the basis of true wisdom. It is the solid foundation on which a person can base a way of life that will lead to blessings in time and in eternity. These blessings are described more fully in the next psalm.

# Psalm 112

### *The man who fears the Lord*

¹ Praise the LORD.

Blessed is the man who fears the LORD,
who finds great delight in his commands.
² His children will be mighty in the land;
the generation of the upright will be blessed.
³ Wealth and riches are in his house,
and his righteousness endures forever.
⁴ Even in darkness light dawns for the upright,
for the gracious and compassionate
and righteous man.
⁵ Good will come to him
who is generous and lends freely,
who conducts his affairs with justice.
⁶ Surely he will never be shaken;
a righteous man will be remembered forever.

⁷He will have no fear of bad news;
his heart is steadfast, trusting in the L<small>ORD</small>.
⁸His heart is secure,
he will have no fear;
in the end he will look in triumph on his foes.
⁹He has scattered abroad his gifts to the poor,
his righteousness endures forever;
his horn will be lifted high in honor.

¹⁰ The wicked man will see and be vexed,
he will gnash his teeth and waste away;
the longings of the wicked will come to nothing.

Psalm 112 lists some of the characteristics of the upright man. He fears the Lord, that is, he believes, respects, and obeys God's Word. He finds pleasure in obeying God's Word. His righteousness is described in the same terms as the Lord's: gracious, compassionate, and enduring forever (compare Psalms 111:3,4 and 112:3,4).

This comparison suggests that his righteousness is patterned after God's. The righteous man is generous with his possessions and just in his dealings. His spiritual and material blessings complement each other, because the spiritual attitudes enable him to use the material possessions wisely, and the material possessions enable him to practice the spiritual attitudes.

The psalm also lists some of the blessings the upright person receives. He has wealth and riches. This may include abundant earthly possessions and the right attitude for enjoying them. Even if these are lost, he still possesses the true riches of a right relationship with God and the confidence of eternal salvation. This permits him to be happy even in dark days and times of trouble.

He doesn't have to fear bad news and reverses because he knows how his story is going to turn out in the end. He will stand with God in honor and glory when the final victory has been won and Christ's eternal kingdom has appeared. He can also look to the future on earth with confidence, since he knows his children have a bright future if they cling to the heritage of God's Word, which he leaves to them.

This psalm is a good text for a study of Christian attitudes toward possessions. It warns against the temptations that riches bring: selfishness, fear of the future, and abuse of power. It urges the Christian to practice generosity and contentment. Paul quotes from this psalm in 2 Corinthians 9:9, which is part of his well-known discussion of stewardship.

The psalm closes with a brief contrasting view of the future of the ungodly man. No matter what prosperity and power he may enjoy for a while, he will come to grief in the end. His greatest grief will be the eternal awareness of the blessings from which he has excluded himself.

# Psalms 113–118

### *The Passover hallel*

The main occasions for Israel to remember and ponder God's works and Word were the three pilgrimage festivals, especially the Passover. According to Jewish tradition, Psalms 113 to 118 became a standard part of the Passover celebrations. Psalms 113 and 114 were used before the meal, and Psalms 116 to 118 were used after the meal. These psalms are often called the Passover hallel or Egyptian hallel. *Hallel* means "praise."

# Psalm 113

### *The mighty deliverer*

Psalm 113 is connected with Psalms 111 and 112 by the introductory "Praise the Lord" (hallelujah). It is an apt introduction to the Passover collection, because it describes the mighty God, who accomplished the Passover deliverance.

> ¹ Praise the LORD.
>
> Praise, O servants of the LORD,
> praise the name of the LORD.
> ²Let the name of the LORD be praised,
> both now and forevermore.
> ³From the rising of the sun
> to the place where it sets,
> the name of the LORD is to be praised.
>
> ⁴ The LORD is exalted over all the nations,
> his glory above the heavens.
> ⁵Who is like the LORD our God,
> the One who sits enthroned on high,
> ⁶who stoops down to look on the heavens
> and the earth?
> ⁷He raises the poor from the dust
> and lifts the needy from the ash heap;
> ⁸he seats them with princes,
> with the princes of their people.
> ⁹He settles the barren woman in her home
> as a happy mother of children.
>
> Praise the LORD.

Psalm 113 provides a general description of the Lord as the deliverer. Psalm 114 will provide the specific application to the Passover and exodus.

The first section of this psalm invites everyone to praise the Lord. He deserves to be praised at all times and in every place.

The second part of the psalm provides the basis for this invitation. The Lord should be praised for who he is. He is the one and only God. He is so high above us that he must bend down to see the sky. He is the ruler of all nations and should be served by all of them. He is incomparable and deserves incomparable praise.

The Lord should be praised for what he does. He is both far above us and very near to us. Although he is lofty in power and majesty, he uses that power to help his people. The description of the Lord's help for the lowly is adapted from the song of Hannah in 1 Samuel chapter 2; verses 7 and 8 correspond very closely to 1 Samuel 2:8. God made barren Hannah a happy mother of children. This experience is reflected in verse 5 of Hannah's song and verse 9 of the psalm.

This general principle, that God helps the lowly among his people, found an outstanding fulfillment when the Lord led the Israelites out of slavery in Egypt and made them the rulers of a good land. It found an even more outstanding example when God's Son was born of a virgin. The song of Mary in Luke chapter 1 echoes the theme of Hannah's song. God sends his Son down to us so that we can be raised up to life with him. Nothing is too great for him to accomplish; no one is too lowly to receive his help.

# Psalm 114

## *When Israel came out of Egypt*

Psalm 114 makes the specific application to the exodus of the principle expressed in Psalm 113. It portrays the exodus and conquest as earthshaking displays of the Lord's power.

¹When Israel came out of Egypt,
 the house of Jacob from a people of foreign tongue,
²Judah became God's sanctuary,
 Israel his dominion.

³The sea looked and fled,
 the Jordan turned back;
⁴the mountains skipped like rams,
 the hills like lambs.

⁵Why was it, O sea, that you fled,
 O Jordan, that you turned back,
⁶you mountains, that you skipped like rams,
 you hills, like lambs?

⁷Tremble, O earth, at the presence of the Lord,
 at the presence of the God of Jacob,
⁸who turned the rock into a pool,
 the hard rock into springs of water.

The purpose of the exodus and conquest was not simply to found another nation. It was to establish the nation in which God's Word would be preserved and in which his temple would be built. Though Israel was never great among the nations in earthly terms, the founding of Israel was nevertheless an earthshaking event, for the Savior, the ruler of the universe, would arise from Israel. God's use of Israel to bring salvation to the world was an example of his use of the lowly to accomplish great things.

The skipping of the mountains and fearful flight of the sea are poetic ways of describing the awesome power of God, which makes the whole earth tremble. The events in Egypt and at the crossing of the Jordan filled the Canaanites with fear of Israel. God's miraculous provision of water in the wilderness also demonstrated his love and care for his

people. All of these acts should move the peoples to recognize the Lord as the only God and to praise his name.

Some commentators believe that the skipping of the hills
is a description of the method by which God opened a path
through the Jordan. Joshua chapter 3 tells us that the Jordan
stopped flowing far upstream from Israel's crossing point.
This has led some people to suggest that God used an
earthquake to block the flow of the Jordan till Israel
crossed. God does sometimes use natural phenomena in
performing his miracles, but since nothing is mentioned
about such an earthquake in Joshua chapter 3, it seems best
to regard the language of Psalm 114 as figurative.

By its striking personification, this psalm expresses the
awe that even the inanimate creation experiences in the
presence of its Creator. This is expressed in a more positive
way in Psalms 96 and 97. Psalm 46 describes the tumult that
heaven and earth, land and sea will undergo when the
judge appears. If even the universe stands in awe before its
Creator and preserver, how much more so should man.

Like the preceding psalm, Psalm 114 ends on a quiet
note, which expresses God's love and care for his people.

# Psalm 115

### *Not unto us*

Although this psalm does not mention the exodus, it nevertheless is appropriate for use at the Passover because of its
emphasis on corporate praise and its recognition that all the
glory for the exodus and conquest belonged to the Lord alone.

*To God alone be glory*

> ¹ Not to us, O LORD, not to us
> but to your name be the glory,
> because of your love and faithfulness.

174

The great Passover celebration in the beautiful temple in Jerusalem could very easily tempt Israel to pride. What a great nation we are! What marvelous victories we have won! What a beautiful temple we have built! The opening verse of this psalm puts a damper on such pride. Not to us, not to us, but to your name be the glory!

The Israelites did nothing to compel Pharaoh to release them. They did nothing to help Moses provide for them in the wilderness. They were more of a hindrance than a help. Their history is a story of the Lord's love and faithfulness. They were unfaithful, but he remained true to the covenant he had given to Abraham. They were weak, but he was mighty. The one and only God made them what they were. He alone deserved the praise.

For obvious reasons we often use this verse on such occasions as church anniversaries. It reminds us not to glory in our accomplishments but to give glory to the Lord, who has given us all we have. When we contemplate the facilities of our church and our works of faith, we too say, "Not unto us, not unto us, but to your name be the glory."

## No glory in idols

> ²**Why do the nations say,**
>   **"Where is their God?"**
>
> ³ **Our God is in heaven;**
>   **he does whatever pleases him.**
>
> ⁴ **But their idols are silver and gold,**
>   **made by the hands of men.**
> ⁵**They have mouths, but cannot speak,**
>   **eyes, but they cannot see;**
> ⁶**they have ears, but cannot hear,**
>   **noses, but they cannot smell;**

⁷they have hands, but cannot feel,
  feet, but they cannot walk;
  nor can they utter a sound with their throats.
⁸Those who make them will be like them,
  and so will all who trust in them.

God's people do not always live in the midst of triumph and celebration. There may be dark days of testing, when events do not seem to justify their faith. It was such a day when Pharaoh said, "Who is the Lord that I should obey him?" It was such a day when the proud king of Assyria said, "No god has stopped me yet, and the Lord won't either." It was such a day when the arrogant Nebuchadnezzar carried off the people of Judah.

But the idols of Egypt and the magicians who served them were helpless to stop the plagues. The gods of Assyria could not stop the angel of death, who marched through Sennacherib's army. The images in the temple of Babylon could not prevent the fall of the city. They were carried away as booty when the city was looted.

In the end Israel could say, "Our God is in heaven; he does whatever pleases him" (verse 3). He sends times of testing to his people when they need it, and he sends deliverance whenever the time is right.

On the other hand, the idols of the nations are simply lifeless creations of their worshipers. This is true whether they are carved images or idols of human philosophy, human achievements, and earthly wealth. None of these will be able to give life to those who serve them. Their worshipers will become as dead as the gods they serve. But those who trust in the Lord will be blessed.

## Trust in the Lord

⁹O house of Israel, trust in the LORD—
  he is their help and shield.

¹⁰O house of Aaron, trust in the L<small>ORD</small>—
   he is their help and shield.
¹¹You who fear him, trust in the L<small>ORD</small>—
   he is their help and shield.

¹²The L<small>ORD</small> remembers us and will bless us:
   He will bless the house of Israel,
   he will bless the house of Aaron,
¹³he will bless those who fear the L<small>ORD</small>—
   small and great alike.

¹⁴May the L<small>ORD</small> make you increase,
   both you and your children.
¹⁵May you be blessed by the L<small>ORD</small>,
   the Maker of heaven and earth.

This section is rich with liturgical repetition. The words that stand out are "trust" and "bless." This is appropriate because there is a just-as-day-follows-night relationship between these concepts. Those who trust in the Lord will be blessed.

Verses 9 to 11 call on all Israel, laypeople and priests alike, to trust the Lord. The term "those who fear the Lord" is probably an inclusive name for the whole people of Israel. However, in later times it became a standard term for the non-Israelites who had come to faith in the true God, and it could have that meaning here.

For all who trust him, the Lord is a help and shield. The middle verses of this section emphatically state the reality of the Lord's blessing upon all who trust in him, whether small or great.

The closing verses pray for God's blessing on the whole people, present and future. This blessing is certain, because the Lord is the maker of heaven and earth, who controls all things.

*Serve the Lord*

>  ¹⁶ **The highest heavens belong to the L**ORD**,**
>  **but the earth he has given to man.**
>
>  ¹⁷ **It is not the dead who praise the L**ORD**,**
>  **those who go down to silence;**
>  ¹⁸ **it is we who extol the L**ORD**,**
>  **both now and forevermore.**
>
>  **Praise the L**ORD**.**

Although God made everything and has given us all we have, this does not leave us without responsibility. We are to be faithful stewards of the earth, which he has entrusted to our care, particularly to the specific portions of its resources that he has given to us as individuals. We are to make full use of the time he has given us on this earth, to spread the glory of his name before our opportunity to do so is ended by death. But even when death ends our responsibility and opportunity to serve God on this earth, we will continue to praise him forever. Then, as now, we will praise the Lord for his love and faithfulness.

# Psalm 116

### *Deliverance from death*

Psalm 116 seems to be rather loosely related to the Passover theme of the surrounding psalms. It is an individual's thanks for deliverance from death. It can be related to the sparing of the firstborn in Egypt, or "death" may also be understood as an expression for the plight of the nation in Egypt. The psalm does not have a distinct progression of parts but circles around its theme several times.

Although this psalm is not quoted in the New Testament as a messianic psalm, nevertheless, because the whole Passover experience points to the work of Christ, it is appropriate to see this psalm as a reflection of Christ's confidence that he would be delivered from death.

*Overview*

> ¹I love the LORD,
> for he heard my voice;
> he heard my cry for mercy.
> ²Because he turned his ear to me,
> I will call on him
> as long as I live.
>
> ³The cords of death entangled me,
> the anguish of the grave came upon me;
> I was overcome by trouble and sorrow.
>
> ⁴Then I called on the name of the LORD:
> "O LORD, save me!"
>
> ⁵The LORD is gracious and righteous;
> our God is full of compassion.
> ⁶The LORD protects the simplehearted;
> when I was in great need, he saved me.

The first two verses already tell the story of the psalm. The psalmist is devoted to thanking the Lord because the Lord has delivered him from danger. By remembering the past, he receives assurance and dedication for the present and the future. The closing verses of this section elaborate on the details. The psalmist was in great danger of death; he prayed to the Lord; the Lord saved him. That, in brief, is the story of this psalm. The following sections also elaborate on the details of the psalmist's deliverance.

## Past deliverance

> <sup>7</sup> **Be at rest once more, O my soul,**
>   **for the LORD has been good to you.**
> <sup>8</sup> **For you, O LORD, have delivered my soul from death,**
>   **my eyes from tears, my feet from stumbling,**
> <sup>9</sup> **that I may walk before the LORD**
>         **in the land of the living.**
> <sup>10</sup> **I believed; therefore I said,**
>   **"I am greatly afflicted."**
> <sup>11</sup> **And in my dismay I said,**
>   **"All men are liars."**

The psalmist briefly reviews the help he received from the Lord. He was delivered from the physical danger of death and also from the spiritual danger of excessive grief and uncertainty, which tried his faith. Death and the grave had been like relentless enemies who carried him to the brink of despair. He had felt crushed by great affliction. His distress was apparently made worse by false accusers, who implied that he was getting the punishment his sins deserved. He realized that he could not count on men to help, so he turned to the Lord alone.

In 2 Corinthians 4:13 Paul uses the Greek form of verse 10, "I believed; therefore I have spoken," as a statement of the motivation for his proclamation of the gospel. Some have questioned the appropriateness of Paul's quotation, since in the psalm these words introduce a complaint, not a gospel proclamation. However, this is one of those New Testament citations of an Old Testament passage that are intended to refer not only to the words quoted but to the whole context that surrounds them.

Paul's point in 2 Corinthians chapter 4 is that he preaches boldly and willingly because the Lord has delivered him from danger and death. This is exactly the same point being made by the psalmist in Psalm 116, so Paul's reference to the psalm is very appropriate. Both Paul and the psalmist were sustained and motivated by faith. Like Paul, the psalmist was delivered for a purpose, so that he could walk before the Lord in the land of the living.

## *Future devotion*

<sup>12</sup> How can I repay the LORD
   for all his goodness to me?
<sup>13</sup> I will lift up the cup of salvation
   and call on the name of the LORD.
<sup>14</sup> I will fulfill my vows to the LORD
      in the presence of all his people.

<sup>15</sup> Precious in the sight of the LORD
      is the death of his saints.

<sup>16</sup> O LORD, truly I am your servant;
   I am your servant, the son of your maidservant;
   you have freed me from my chains.
<sup>17</sup> I will sacrifice a thank offering to you
   and call on the name of the LORD.
<sup>18</sup> I will fulfill my vows to the LORD
      in the presence of all his people,
         <sup>19</sup> in the courts of the house of the LORD—
      in your midst, O Jerusalem.

Praise the LORD.

The Israelites were freed from the chains of slavery in Egypt for a purpose, so that they could serve the Lord in the land he would give them. We have been freed from the chains of slavery to sin for a purpose, so that we can serve the Lord by proclaiming his glory in the presence of others. We can never repay God in the sense that we can do enough to compensate the Lord adequately for what he has done for us. But we can repay him in the sense that we honor him with love and gratitude, which is an appropriate expression of thanks for what he has done.

We do this when we joyfully celebrate the salvation he has given to us. "Lifting the cup of salvation" is often interpreted as a reference to the cup of wine used at the Passover and other festive meals. This expression may include an allusion to that custom, but it is basically a figurative expression for everything we do that celebrates and proclaims our appreciation for God's salvation. The cup of salvation is God's gift to us. Lifting the cup is our celebration and proclamation of God's gift. The Passover meal was one way Israel remembered and proclaimed God's work of salvation.

Our celebration of the Lord's Supper includes such remembrance and proclamation of Christ's work for our salvation. In fact, all our public worship serves this purpose. One reason we regularly attend public worship is to declare to others our appreciation for salvation. Every act of public worship is a visible sermon that proclaims our thankfulness for all that God has done.

The ancient Israelites often took vows to perform some specific act of thanksgiving if God answered their prayers. We seldom use such vows today. But on the day of our confirmation, we did vow that our lives would be a fitting response of thankfulness for the salvation God has given us. We vowed to be faithful in our use of the Word and sacraments. We vowed to strive to live our lives according to God's Word. We vowed that with God's help we would be faithful even unto death. Let us renew our dedication to fulfilling those vows in the presence of God's people. This is the thank offering by which we can "repay" God's goodness to us.

"Precious in the sight of the LORD is the death of his saints" (verse 15). God cares about the life and death of every sparrow in his creation. How much more he watches over the lives of his saints. He controls the life of each one of us so that its length best serves his glory and our good. He will be with us to help us cross that boundary which is still fearsome to us. Our times are in his hands. Let us wisely use the time he allots us. Let us be ready to entrust ourselves into his hands when he calls us.

# Psalm 117

## *Praise the Lord*

This is the shortest chapter in the Bible. This little psalm is the seventh of the collection of praise psalms that began with Psalm 111. As such, it is probably intended to serve as a doxology and conclusion to the whole group. It briefly reviews and summarizes the content of the whole group.

> [1] **Praise the LORD, all you nations;**
> **extol him, all you peoples.**
> [2] **For great is his love toward us,**
> **and the faithfulness of the LORD endures forever.**
>
> **Praise the LORD.**

This little gem sweeps across space and time. It is for all people. It celebrates love, which is forever.

It is striking that a psalm used at the Passover, Israel's national celebration, is so inclusive. It reminds the Israelites that the Lord is not a God for them alone. He is the one and only God for all people. All people can come to him. All people must come to him. This psalm rejects the popular notion that different cultures and races can have their own religions and that we should leave them undisturbed. There can be a diversity of cultures and languages among those who serve the Lord, but there can be no diversity of gods. There is only one Creator and one Redeemer. All nations are called to serve him.

Paul refers to this psalm in Romans 15:7-13 as a basis for his missionary work among the Gentiles. The opening verse of the psalm is expressed in the form of a command, but it is really an invitation to the nations of the world. To accomplish its purpose, an invitation must be delivered. How can the nations praise and extol the Lord if they have not heard of his love and faithfulness? The answer is obvious. The nations can respond to the Lord's invitation only if we who already have heard it pass it on to others.

We are to pass on the message of God's love and faithfulness. This message is the gospel covenant that God gave first to Adam and Eve, then later to Abraham. The love "for us" includes God's love for Israel through whom the Savior came, and the "for us" broadens out to include all who become children of Abraham through faith in the promised Savior.

The love and faithfulness revealed in the gospel covenant are great. God loved the world so much that he gave his only Son. He made the payment for all our sins and not for ours only but for the sins of the whole world. The love and the faithfulness established by the gospel covenant are eternal. Nothing can change God's plan of salvation. Nothing can overthrow it. His plan stands firm. His plan stands alone. No one who believes the gospel will be lost. No one will be saved in any other way. In Christ, God has provided the sure way of salvation, the only way of salvation. For this great love and faithfulness, the people gathered from all nations will forever sing, "Praise the Lord!"

It is interesting to note that this little psalm, the short-est chapter in the Bible, which is addressed to all the people in the world, is the middle chapter of the Bible.

# Psalm 118

### *The stone the builders rejected*

Psalm 118 is one of the foremost messianic psalms. As the last psalm of the Passover collection, it may have been the last hymn Jesus and the apostles sang on Maundy Thursday evening. If so, it was very fitting, for it contains many references to the events of Holy Week. After its introduction it falls into two main parts: the Mes-siah's expression of trust during his suffering and his joy when God delivers him. Both of these experiences are shared with Christ by the believers who preceded him during the Old Testament era and by those who follow him during the New Testament era.

A notable characteristic of this psalm is the frequent poetic repetition.

### *Introduction*

<sup></sup>
¹Give thanks to the LORD,
 for he is good;
 his love endures forever.

²Let Israel say:
 "His love endures forever."
³Let the house of Aaron say:
 "His love endures forever."
⁴Let those who fear the LORD say:
 "His love endures forever."

This call to thanksgiving is a general invitation that appears also in other psalms. Verse 1 is the refrain of

Psalm 136 and will be discussed in more detail there. Verses 2 and 3 use the same threefold division as Psalm 115:9-13. As they are rearranged here, these verses provide an appropriate introduction to the main body of the psalm, which speaks of the great deeds God performs through and for Christ.

*Trust in distress*

⁵ In my anguish I cried to the LORD,
  and he answered by setting me free.

⁶ The LORD is with me;
  I will not be afraid.
  What can man do to me?
⁷ The LORD is with me;
  he is my helper.
  I will look in triumph on my enemies.

⁸ It is better to take refuge in the LORD
        than to trust in man.
⁹ It is better to take refuge in the LORD
        than to trust in princes.

¹⁰ All the nations surrounded me,
  but in the name of the LORD I cut them off.
¹¹ They surrounded me on every side,
  but in the name of the LORD I cut them off.
¹² They swarmed around me like bees,
  but they died out as quickly as burning thorns;
  in the name of the LORD I cut them off.
¹³ I was pushed back and about to fall,
  but the LORD helped me.

This psalm is fulfilled in Christ's passion. The anguish of the psalm is expressed in Jesus' prayer in Gethsemane and in the words "My God, my God, why have you forsaken me?" (Matthew 27:46). The confidence of the psalm shines through the words "Father, into your hands I commit my spirit" (Luke 23:46). When men failed Jesus, when his disciples deserted him, when the spiritual leaders of Israel who should have been his greatest support were instead his greatest enemies, his Father was with him. Though it seemed his enemies had won, God delivered Jesus from death through his resurrection. On judgment day he will look in triumph on his enemies.

Verses 10 to 12 remind us of the viciousness and persistence of Jesus' enemies, as described in Psalm 22 and in the gospel accounts. Jews and Gentiles joined together to torment him and put him to death. The sins of all the people of the world weighed him down. Though it seemed that he was defeated, the Lord delivered him. We join him in celebrating that victory, for his victory is our victory.

## Joy in victory

> <sup>14</sup>The LORD is my strength and my song;
>   he has become my salvation.
> <sup>15</sup>Shouts of joy and victory resound
>         in the tents of the righteous:
>   "The LORD's right hand has done mighty things!
> <sup>16</sup>The LORD's right hand is lifted high;
>   the LORD's right hand has done mighty things!"
>
> <sup>17</sup>I will not die but live,
>   and will proclaim what the LORD has done.
>
> <sup>18</sup>The LORD has chastened me severely,
>   but he has not given me over to death.
>
> <sup>19</sup>Open for me the gates of righteousness;
>   I will enter and give thanks to the LORD.

²⁰ This is the gate of the LORD
through which the righteous may enter.
²¹ I will give you thanks,
for you answered me;
you have become my salvation.

²² The stone the builders rejected
has become the capstone;
²³ the LORD has done this,
and it is marvelous in our eyes.
²⁴ This is the day the LORD has made;
let us rejoice and be glad in it.

²⁵ O LORD, save us;
O LORD, grant us success.

²⁶ Blessed is he who comes in the name of the LORD.
From the house of the LORD we bless you.

²⁷ The LORD is God,
and he has made his light shine upon us.
With boughs in hand, join in the festal procession
up to the horns of the altar.

²⁸ You are my God, and I will give you thanks;
you are my God, and I will exalt you.

## Conclusion

²⁹ Give thanks to the LORD,
for he is good;
his loves endures forever.

This hymn of thanksgiving alternates between the rejoicing of the Messiah and the rejoicing of his people. In the "I" sections, the Messiah expresses his personal joy; in the "we" sections, believers express the joy we share with him.

Verses 17 to 21 are first of all the words of the Messiah (although we who follow in his footsteps can share them with him). Christ did not remain in death; he rose so that victory and salvation could be proclaimed to all nations. He has reentered heaven, but he continues to proclaim salvation through his people who remain on earth. The salvation he experienced was not forgiveness of sins but deliverance from death and from the guilt of our sins.

Verses 22 to 27 are believers' echoing of the Messiah's joy. Christ is called the "stone the builders rejected" because the leaders of Israel rejected him as the Messiah, even though he was the foundation on whom God would build the church. Whether the "capstone" is the keystone that holds up an arch or the cornerstone around which the building is arranged or the capstone over a door, the picture is the same. The church can be built on nothing else than faith in Christ. We can be part of God's building only through our relationship with Christ. No one can lay any foundation for faith other than the death and resurrection of Christ, which are proclaimed in the Scriptures, written by the prophets and apostles.

Scripture makes much use of this picture of Christ as the stone over whom some stumble and the rock who is a sure foundation for others. Isaiah 28:16 is a further Old Testament development of the positive side of the picture: Christ is a sure foundation. Isaiah 8:14 expresses the negative side of the picture: Christ is a rock of stumbling. In Matthew 21:42 and the parallels in the other gospels, Jesus quotes Psalm 118 as a condemnation of the leaders' rejection of him. In Acts 4:11 Peter makes the same application of the passage. In the second chapter of his first letter, Peter brings together all three Old Testament references in a comprehensive treatment of the theme.

The hosanna sung on Palm Sunday is based on verses 25 and 26 of this psalm. This song has entered into the traditions of Christian worship as part of the Sanctus of the Communion liturgy. *Hosanna* is a Hebrew form of the word translated "save us" in the NIV rendering of verse 25. This expression was joined together with the words "Blessed is he who comes in the name of the LORD" to form the core of the Palm Sunday hymn. The people of Jesus' day must have recognized the messianic implications of Psalm 118 when they used it to welcome Jesus as the Messiah.

Since the "you" of the second half of verse 26 is plural in Hebrew, it is apparently not a continuation of the people's blessing on Christ, but a blessing on those who join them in following Christ.

Although some portions of verse 27 are difficult to translate, the general picture is clear. The act of welcoming Christ is described in terms borrowed from the custom of carrying branches in the procession to the temple during the Feast of Tabernacles. This custom was fulfilled literally during the parade welcoming Jesus on Palm Sunday. Its deeper implications are fulfilled whenever we joyfully celebrate Christ's work. It will be fulfilled again when we welcome Jesus on his return to the earth, just as the crowds welcomed him on Palm Sunday.

Verse 29 seems to be a return to the words of the Messiah. It is fitting that he, as the leader of the people, should bring this outburst of praise to its conclusion.

The final verse of the psalm is like parentheses enclosing it as it began.

This psalm is a glorious hymn celebrating the triumph of God's people under the leadership of the king whom God sends to them. It was fulfilled in dim foreshadowings when David completed the long journey from Sinai to Zion by establishing Jerusalem as the City of God. Its true fulfillment burst into the open in the spontaneous, enthusiastic singing on the road into Jerusalem on Palm Sunday. The cycle of praise that began then will reach its climax when we join the festive procession into the heavenly Jerusalem.

# Psalm 119

### *The law of the Lord*

Psalm 119 is the longest psalm and the longest chapter in the Bible. Additional factors that make it difficult for modern readers to appreciate this psalm are its poetic technique and its repetitious style, both of which are foreign to our tastes. For this reason the presentation of Psalm 119 will depart from the normal format of this commentary. The psalm will be introduced with some extensive comments on its style and message. We hope these will assist the reader in studying and appreciating the psalm. Then the psalm itself will be presented with relatively little comment.

### *Poetic form*

Psalm 119 is an elaborate acrostic. The term *acrostic* refers to a literary technique in which the writer uses the first letter or first word of a series of poetic units to form a significant pattern or to spell out a message. The unit that begins with an acrostic sign may be a line, the first of a pair of lines or of a triplet of lines, or even the first line of a stanza or paragraph. The two major types of acrostics are *sequence* acrostics, in which the first letters of the lines fulfill a fixed sequence, such as the order of the alphabet, and *message* acrostics, in which the acrostic letters spell out a message. There are no message acrostics in the Bible. All biblical acrostics are alphabetic sequences.

Psalm 119 carries the complete alphabetic acrostic to its extreme. Each of the 22 letters of the Hebrew alphabet is represented by an eight-verse stanza. All eight verses of each stanza begin with the appropriate sequential letter. The heading of each stanza in the NIV text is the name of the Hebrew letter with which each line of that stanza begins. For example, all eight verses of the first stanza begin with the letter *aleph,* all eight verses of the second stanza with *beth,* and so on.

Each verse is printed as a single line in the Hebrew text, but in English translation the length of the verses requires that they be divided into two lines, as is done in the arrangement of the text in this commentary. Sometimes the second line of the verse forms a parallelism with the first line. Sometimes it is simply a continuation or elaboration of the thought of the first line. These second lines of the verse do not start with the acrostic letter.

The main purpose of this poetic technique is to express completeness. The psalmist wants to meditate carefully on every aspect of God's Word "from A to Z." Unfortunately, this acrostic technique, which made the psalm a beautifully expressive poem to the original readers, is entirely lost in our translations. It is no wonder, then, that Psalm 119 is less appealing to us than it was to them, since we have lost its most important poetic feature.

## Content

We also have difficulty with the content of Psalm 119 because of its repetitiousness. Psalm 119 is a meditation on the characteristics and blessings of God's law. Eight distinct terms for God's law appear repeatedly throughout the psalm. This selection of terms may explain the eightfold repetition of each letter in the psalm. However, although each line of the poem normally includes one of these eight names of the law, all eight names do not appear systematically in each eight-line stanza. Only six stanzas include all eight terms. No stanza contains fewer than six of the terms. Occasionally other terms for the Word appear.

The eight Hebrew terms and their English equivalents follow:

| | |
|---|---|
| *Torah* (law) | *Torah* means "instruction." It is not limited to commands but includes all of God's Word, both law and gospel. |
| *Edot* (testimonies, statutes) | *Edot* emphasizes the witnessing character of God's Word. |
| *Piqqudim* (precepts) | *Piqqudim* describes God's Word as the supervisor of our lives. |
| *Huqqim* (statutes, decrees) | *Huqqim* describes the binding nature and the established permanence of the Word. |
| *Mitzvot* (commandments, commands) | *Mitzvot* emphasizes the authority of the Word. |
| *Mishpatim* (judgments, laws) | The rulings and statements of God's Word have binding power over us. |
| *Davar* (word) | *Davar* is a general term for everything God has spoken. |
| *Imra* (word, promise) | *Imra* is a poetic synonym of *davar* but is translated as "promise" for variety. |

Although each of these words has a different emphasis, these words are not used distinctly in the psalm. Generally they are used as synonyms. The main reason for using one or the other is simply for variety.

Although Psalm 119 seems rambling and disorganized to many present-day readers, it has a definite progression of thought. The psalmist moves from a concern for God's law (stanzas *Aleph* to *He)* to his own distress *(Waw* to *Kaph),* then back to God's law *(Lamedh* to *Nun),* then to distress at the wickedness of God's enemies *(Samekh* to *Tsadhe),* and finally to a closing pledge of obedience *(Qoph* to *Taw).* In spite of this limited amount of progression of thought, it must be admitted that the psalmist circles freely around a number of topics, rather than follows an outline, as we do in modern Western style.

The psalm includes no distinct indications of date or authorship. It has often been classified as postexilic, but it has many common characteristics with the psalms of the first two books of Psalms, which are mostly from the time of David. It appears to be an elaboration of a portion of Psalm 19, which is by David. There is nothing to justify the critics' contention that the acrostic is a late, postexilic, literary form, since the closest parallel to biblical acrostics is found in Egyptian poems from about 1200 B.C.

## Suggestions for reading

We live in an age not much given to meditation. People are in a hurry. People have short attention spans. They want a lot of action in their entertainment, and they often expect their worship to be the same. It is, therefore, not surprising that Psalm 119 is not very popular with present-day readers. Studying Psalm 119 requires patience. Appreciating

Psalm 119 requires meditation. As you read it, remember that the great truths of God's Word are worth saying more than once. They are worth thinking about.

As you read the psalm, try to pick out the repetition of these five themes:

## 1. God's Word as law and gospel

The psalm often speaks of the rebuking, correcting, and condemning power of the Word. This is law. The psalm often speaks of the life-giving power of the Word. This is gospel.

## 2. Characteristics of the Word

The psalmist emphasizes that the Word is righteous, dependable, unshakeable, and limitless.

## 3. Attitudes toward God's law

The psalmist finds *delight* in the law. We get our joy primarily from the gospel, but because we have been renewed in the image of God by the Holy Spirit, we also *love* God's commandments. They are not a burden to us. We love God's Word because we find our Savior there. Today when so many people ridicule an inerrant Bible as a "paper pope," we do well to cling to the same devotion to the Word expressed by the psalmist.

## 4. Blessings of the Word

God's Word gives us *life* through the forgiving power of the gospel. The Word gives us *freedom*. It not only frees us from sin but gives us the power to begin serving God, which is true freedom. God's Word gives us *light* (*light* represents both joy and guidance). God's Word gives us *stability* so that we are not pulled in every direction by pressure from people of the world.

## 5. The enemies of the Word

The psalmist faces much opposition from the enemies of the Word. He expresses both sorrow and indignation at their scorn for the Word. He is determined to oppose them and to cling to the Word.

As you read the psalm, mark verses that are good expressions of the five themes listed. Mark other verses that strike you as being especially meaningful or useful for various occasions in life. The headline under the title of each section is intended to help draw your attention to passages that catch the flavor of each stanza.

As you read the psalm, try to find there the joy, love, and devotion for God's Word that the psalmist found.

# Part 1

Stanzas *Aleph* through *He* emphasize the guidance believers receive from the Word. The first three stanzas also serve as an introduction to the whole psalm.

א *Aleph—blessed are they*

¹ Blessed are they whose ways are blameless,
who walk according to the law of the LORD.
² Blessed are they who keep his statutes
and seek him with all their heart.
³ They do nothing wrong;
they walk in his ways.
⁴ You have laid down precepts
that are to be fully obeyed.
⁵ Oh, that my ways were steadfast
in obeying your decrees!
⁶ Then I would not be put to shame
when I consider all your commands.
⁷ I will praise you with an upright heart
as I learn your righteous laws.
⁸ I will obey your decrees;
do not utterly forsake me.

The opening word, "Blessed," links Psalm 119 with Psalm 1, which has the same theme as Psalm 119 but is much more limited in scope. The complete devotion that God's Word deserves is expressed in such phrases as "all their heart" and "fully obeyed." In verse 7 the psalmist confesses that although he is devoted to the Word, he still has much to learn.

## ב *Beth—hidden in my heart*

⁹**How can a young man keep his way pure?**
  **By living according to your word.**
¹⁰**I seek you with all my heart;**
  **do not let me stray from your commands.**
¹¹**I have hidden your word in my heart**
  **that I might not sin against you.**
¹²**Praise be to you, O LORD;**
  **teach me your decrees.**
¹³**With my lips I recount all the laws**
  **that come from your mouth.**
¹⁴**I rejoice in following your statutes**
  **as one rejoices in great riches.**
¹⁵**I meditate on your precepts**
  **and consider your ways.**
¹⁶**I delight in your decrees;**
  **I will not neglect your word.**

God's Word should be read, studied, meditated upon, and memorized, so that it is hidden in our hearts for use whenever we need it.

## ג *Gimel—open my eyes*

¹⁷**Do good to your servant, and I will live;**
  **I will obey your word.**
¹⁸**Open my eyes that I may see**
  **wonderful things in your law.**
¹⁹**I am a stranger on earth;**
  **do not hide your commands from me.**
²⁰**My soul is consumed with longing**
  **for your laws at all times.**

²¹ You rebuke the arrogant, who are cursed
and who stray from your commands.
²² Remove from me scorn and contempt,
for I keep your statutes.
²³ Though rulers sit together and slander me,
your servant will meditate on your decrees.
²⁴ Your statutes are my delight;
they are my counselors.

ヿ  *Daleth—a free heart*

²⁵ I am laid low in the dust;
preserve my life according to your word.
²⁶ I recounted my ways and you answered me;
teach me your decrees.
²⁷ Let me understand the teaching of your precepts;
then I will meditate on your wonders.
²⁸ My soul is weary with sorrow;
strengthen me according to your word.
²⁹ Keep me from deceitful ways;
be gracious to me through your law.
³⁰ I have chosen the way of truth;
I have set my heart on your laws.
³¹ I hold fast to your statutes, O LORD;
do not let me be put to shame.
³² I run in the path of your commands,
for you have set my heart free.

*Gimel* and *Daleth* first introduce the stress the psalmist experiences because of the opposition of the enemies. A number of verses in these two stanzas, culminating in verse 32, state a truth repeated throughout the psalm: only the Lord can give us understanding of his Word and the ability to believe and obey it.

ה *He—that you may be feared*

³³ Teach me, O LORD, to follow your decrees;
   then I will keep them to the end.
³⁴ Give me understanding, and I will keep your law
   and obey it with all my heart.
³⁵ Direct me in the path of your commands,
   for there I find delight.
³⁶ Turn my heart toward your statutes
   and not toward selfish gain.
³⁷ Turn my eyes away from worthless things;
   preserve my life according to your word.
³⁸ Fulfill your promise to your servant,
   so that you may be feared.
³⁹ Take away the disgrace I dread,
   for your laws are good.
⁴⁰ How I long for your precepts!
   Preserve my life in your righteousness.

Verses 36 and 37 are noteworthy as a prayer for God-pleasing values and priorities in life.

# Part 2

Although there is not a strict differentiation of subject matter between parts of the psalm, in stanzas *Waw* to *Kaph* there is more emphasis on the suffering of the psalmist than in the preceding sections.

ו *Waw—speak before kings*

⁴¹ May your unfailing love come to me, O LORD,
   your salvation according to your promise;
⁴² then I will answer the one who taunts me,
   for I trust in your word.
⁴³ Do not snatch the word of truth from my mouth,
   for I have put my hope in your laws.

<sup>44</sup>I will always obey your law,
   for ever and ever.
<sup>45</sup>I will walk about in freedom,
   for I have sought out your precepts.
<sup>46</sup>I will speak of your statutes before kings
   and will not be put to shame,
<sup>47</sup>for I delight in your commands
   because I love them.
<sup>48</sup>I lift up my hands to your commands, which I love,
   and I meditate on your decrees.

Verse 46 was very meaningful to Luther and the other reformers when they were summoned to appear before the emperor and princes. It also must have been very comforting to the early Christians during days of persecution.

## ז *Zayin—comfort in suffering*

<sup>49</sup>Remember your word to your servant,
   for you have given me hope.
<sup>50</sup>My comfort in my suffering is this:
   Your promise preserves my life.
<sup>51</sup>The arrogant mock me without restraint,
   but I do not turn from your law.
<sup>52</sup>I remember your ancient laws, O Lord,
   and I find comfort in them.
<sup>53</sup>Indignation grips me because of the wicked,
   who have forsaken your law.
<sup>54</sup>Your decrees are the theme of my song
   wherever I lodge.
<sup>55</sup>In the night I remember your name, O Lord,
   and I will keep your law.
<sup>56</sup>This has been my practice:
   I obey your precepts.

ח *Heth—I will not forget*

[57] **You are my portion, O LORD;**
   **I have promised to obey your words.**
[58] **I have sought your face with all my heart;**
   **be gracious to me according to your promise.**
[59] **I have considered my ways**
   **and have turned my steps to your statutes.**
[60] **I will hasten and not delay**
   **to obey your commands.**
[61] **Though the wicked bind me with ropes,**
   **I will not forget your law.**
[62] **At midnight I rise to give you thanks**
   **for your righteous laws.**
[63] **I am a friend to all who fear you,**
   **to all who follow your precepts.**
[64] **The earth is filled with your love,**
   **O LORD; teach me your decrees.**

Verse 57 reminds us of our confirmation pledge. Verse 63 reminds us of the importance of strengthening one another through the practice of Christian fellowship.

ט *Teth—good to be afflicted*

[65] **Do good to your servant**
   **according to your word, O LORD.**
[66] **Teach me knowledge and good judgment,**
   **for I believe in your commands.**
[67] **Before I was afflicted I went astray,**
   **but now I obey your word.**
[68] **You are good, and what you do is good;**
   **teach me your decrees.**
[69] **Though the arrogant have smeared me with lies,**
   **I keep your precepts with all my heart.**
[70] **Their hearts are callous and unfeeling,**
   **but I delight in your law.**

⁷¹ It was good for me to be afflicted
   so that I might learn your decrees.
⁷² The law from your mouth is more precious to me
   than thousands of pieces of silver and gold.

*Teth* emphasizes the disciplinary value suffering may have for a Christian if it pushes him closer to God and his Word.

**י** *Yodh—those who fear you*

⁷³ Your hands made me and formed me;
   give me understanding to learn your commands.
⁷⁴ May those who fear you rejoice when they see me,
   for I have put my hope in your word.
⁷⁵ I know, O LORD, that your laws are righteous,
   and in faithfulness you have afflicted me.
⁷⁶ May your unfailing love be my comfort,
   according to your promise to your servant.
⁷⁷ Let your compassion come to me that I may live,
   for your law is my delight.
⁷⁸ May the arrogant be put to shame
   for wronging me without cause;
   but I will meditate on your precepts.
⁷⁹ May those who fear you turn to me,
   those who understand your statutes.
⁸⁰ May my heart be blameless toward your decrees,
   that I may not be put to shame.

*Yodh* emphasizes the solidarity between the psalmist and all others who fear the Lord. He hopes that his example will encourage them and that they will help and support him.

**כ** *Kaph—a wineskin in the smoke*

⁸¹ My soul faints with longing for your salvation,
   but I have put my hope in your word.

⁸²My eyes fail, looking for your promise;
  I say, "When will you comfort me?"
⁸³Though I am like a wineskin in the smoke,
  I do not forget your decrees.
⁸⁴How long must your servant wait?
  When will you punish my persecutors?
⁸⁵The arrogant dig pitfalls for me,
  contrary to your law.
⁸⁶All your commands are trustworthy;
  help me, for men persecute me without cause.
⁸⁷They almost wiped me from the earth,
  but I have not forsaken your precepts.
⁸⁸Preserve my life according to your love,
  and I will obey the statutes of your mouth.

This section, which focuses on suffering, concludes with a fervent plea for delivery. A wineskin in the smoke becomes shriveled up, cracked, and useless. We would probably say something like "I feel as if I've been through a wringer." In spite of his exhaustion, the psalmist clings to his trust in the Lord.

# Part 3

Stanzas *Lamedh* through *Nun* emphasize the value and purity of the Word. They contain some of the most familiar passages in Psalm 119.

ל *Lamedh—your commands are boundless*

⁸⁹Your word, O Lord, is eternal;
  it stands firm in the heavens.
⁹⁰Your faithfulness continues
      through all generations;
  you established the earth, and it endures.
⁹¹Your laws endure to this day,
  for all things serve you.

⁹² If your law had not been my delight,
  I would have perished in my affliction.
⁹³ I will never forget your precepts,
  for by them you have preserved my life.
⁹⁴ Save me, for I am yours;
  I have sought out your precepts.
⁹⁵ The wicked are waiting to destroy me,
  but I will ponder your statutes.
⁹⁶ To all perfection I see a limit;
  but your commands are boundless.

God's Word is limitless; it is for all people through all time. When heaven and earth pass away, God's Word will remain. Even in eternity we will be living in fulfillment of what it says. God's Word also is limitless in its perfection. All purely human work is subject to error, but the inspired Word is free from such limitations.

## ב  *Mem—sweeter than honey*

⁹⁷ Oh, how I love your law!
  I meditate on it all day long.
⁹⁸ Your commands make me wiser than my enemies,
  for they are ever with me.
⁹⁹ I have more insight than all my teachers,
  for I meditate on your statutes.
¹⁰⁰ I have more understanding than the elders,
  for I obey your precepts.
¹⁰¹ I have kept my feet from every evil path
  so that I might obey your word.
¹⁰² I have not departed from your laws,
  for you yourself have taught me.
¹⁰³ How sweet are your words to my taste,
  sweeter than honey to my mouth!
¹⁰⁴ I gain understanding from your precepts;
  therefore I hate every wrong path.

This is one of the most noteworthy stanzas of the psalm. It expresses both the psalmist's love for the Word and the pleasure he finds in it ("sweeter than honey"). The person who follows the simple truths of the Word is wiser and has more insight and understanding than those who follow the most sophisticated theories of men. A fuller exposition of this principle is found in 1 Corinthians chapters 1 and 2.

Dedication to the truth requires avoidance of evil (verse 101); it also requires opposition to evil (verse 104).

## נ *Nun—a lamp to my feet*

<sup>105</sup> Your word is a lamp to my feet
and a light for my path.
<sup>106</sup> I have taken an oath and confirmed it,
that I will follow your righteous laws.
<sup>107</sup> I have suffered much;
preserve my life, O LORD, according to your word.

<sup>108</sup> Accept, O LORD, the willing praise of my mouth,
and teach me your laws.
<sup>109</sup> Though I constantly take my life in my hands,
I will not forget your law.
<sup>110</sup> The wicked have set a snare for me,
but I have not strayed from your precepts.
<sup>111</sup> Your statutes are my heritage forever;
they are the joy of my heart.
<sup>112</sup> My heart is set on keeping your decrees
to the very end.

Verse 105 is the most famous verse of this lengthy psalm. Many of us memorized it in catechism class as a statement of the value of God's Word as a guide for our lives.

# Part 4

Verse 110 of stanza *Nun* prepared the way for the psalmist's return to a denunciation of his enemies. Stanzas *Samekh* through *Tsadhe* express his indignation against the enemies of the Word.

ס  *Samekh—away from me, evildoers*

<sup>113</sup> I hate double-minded men,
but I love your law.
<sup>114</sup> You are my refuge and my shield;
I have put my hope in your word.
<sup>115</sup> Away from me, you evildoers,
that I may keep the commands of my God!
<sup>116</sup> Sustain me according to your promise,
and I will live;
do not let my hopes be dashed.
<sup>117</sup> Uphold me, and I will be delivered;
I will always have regard for your decrees.
<sup>118</sup> You reject all who stray from your decrees,
for their deceitfulness is in vain.
<sup>119</sup> All the wicked of the earth
you discard like dross;
therefore I love your statutes.
<sup>120</sup> My flesh trembles in fear of you;
I stand in awe of your laws.

ע  *Ayin—it's time to act*

<sup>121</sup> I have done what is righteous and just;
do not leave me to my oppressors.
<sup>122</sup> Ensure your servant's well-being;
let not the arrogant oppress me.
<sup>123</sup> My eyes fail, looking for your salvation,
looking for your righteous promise.
<sup>124</sup> Deal with your servant according to your love
and teach me your decrees.

¹²⁵ I am your servant; give me discernment
    that I may understand your statutes.
¹²⁶ It is time for you to act, O LORD;
    your law is being broken.
¹²⁷ Because I love your commands more than gold,
    more than pure gold,
¹²⁸ and because I consider all your precepts right,
    I hate every wrong path.

פ *Pe—streams of tears*

¹²⁹ Your statutes are wonderful;
    therefore I obey them.
¹³⁰ The unfolding of your words gives light;
    it gives understanding to the simple.
¹³¹ I open my mouth and pant,
    longing for your commands.
¹³² Turn to me and have mercy on me,
    as you always do to those who love your name.
¹³³ Direct my footsteps according to your word;
    let no sin rule over me.
¹³⁴ Redeem me from the oppression of men,
    that I may obey your precepts.
¹³⁵ Make your face shine upon your servant
    and teach me your decrees.
¹³⁶ Streams of tears flow from my eyes,
    for your law is not obeyed.

צ *Tsadhe—my zeal for the Word*

¹³⁷ Righteous are you, O LORD,
    and your laws are right.
¹³⁸ The statutes you have laid down are righteous;
    they are fully trustworthy.
¹³⁹ My zeal wears me out,
    for my enemies ignore your words.

¹⁴⁰ **Your promises have been thoroughly tested,**
    **and your servant loves them.**
¹⁴¹ **Though I am lowly and despised,**
    **I do not forget your precepts.**
¹⁴² **Your righteousness is everlasting**
    **and your law is true.**
¹⁴³ **Trouble and distress have come upon me,**
    **but your commands are my delight.**
¹⁴⁴ **Your statutes are forever right;**
    **give me understanding that I may live.**

In these four stanzas, the psalmist expresses both his
sorrow and indignation over the negligence and scorn many
people show toward the Word. They do not respect the
Lord's authority and power, as the psalmist does (verse 120).
He prays that God will take action against those who scorn
his Word (verse 126) and that he will preserve the psalmist
in his loyalty to the Word (verse 133).

# Part 5

The final four stanzas of the psalm emphasize the commitment of the psalmist to obedience.

ק  *Qoph—I will obey*

¹⁴⁵ **I call with all my heart;**
    **answer me, O LORD, and I will obey your decrees.**
¹⁴⁶ **I call out to you;**
    **save me and I will keep your statutes.**
¹⁴⁷ **I rise before dawn and cry for help;**
    **I have put my hope in your word.**
¹⁴⁸ **My eyes stay open**
            **through the watches of the night,**
    **that I may meditate on your promises.**
¹⁴⁹ **Hear my voice in accordance with your love;**
    **preserve my life, O LORD, according to your laws.**

<sup>150</sup> Those who devise wicked schemes are near,
  but they are far from your law.
<sup>151</sup> Yet you are near, O Lord,
  and all your commands are true.
<sup>152</sup> Long ago I learned from your statutes
  that you established them to last forever.

ר *Resh—I have not forgotten*

<sup>153</sup> Look upon my suffering and deliver me,
  for I have not forgotten your law.
<sup>154</sup> Defend my cause and redeem me;
  preserve my life according to your promise.
<sup>155</sup> Salvation is far from the wicked,
  for they do not seek out your decrees.
<sup>156</sup> Your compassion is great, O Lord,
  preserve my life according to your laws.
<sup>157</sup> Many are the foes who persecute me,
  but I have not turned from your statutes.
<sup>158</sup> I look on the faithless with loathing,
  for they do not obey your word.
<sup>159</sup> See how I love your precepts;
  preserve my life, O Lord, according to your love.

<sup>160</sup> All your words are true;
  all your righteous laws are eternal.

ש *Sin and Shin—I wait for salvation*

<sup>161</sup> Rulers persecute me without cause,
  but my heart trembles at your word.
<sup>162</sup> I rejoice in your promise
  like one who finds great spoil.
<sup>163</sup> I hate and abhor falsehood
  but I love your law.
<sup>164</sup> Seven times a day I praise you
  for your righteous laws.

¹⁶⁵ Great peace have they who love your law,
   and nothing can make them stumble.
¹⁶⁶ I wait for your salvation, O LORD,
   and I follow your commands.
¹⁶⁷ I obey your statutes,
   for I love them greatly.
¹⁶⁸ I obey your precepts and your statutes,
   for all my ways are known to you.

ה *Taw—seek your servant*

¹⁶⁹ May my cry come before you, O LORD;
   give me understanding according to your word.
¹⁷⁰ May my supplication come before you;
   deliver me according to your promise.
¹⁷¹ May my lips overflow with praise,
   for you teach me your decrees.
¹⁷² May my tongue sing of your word,
   for all your commands are righteous.
¹⁷³ May your hand be ready to help me,
   for I have chosen your precepts.
¹⁷⁴ I long for your salvation, O LORD,
   and your law is my delight.
¹⁷⁵ Let me live that I may praise you,
   and may your laws sustain me.
¹⁷⁶ I have strayed like a lost sheep.
   Seek your servant,
   for I have not forgotten your commands.

In the closing stanzas, the psalmist strongly emphasizes his determination to remain faithful to God's Word in spite of the opposition of the enemies of the Word. In the conclusion he returns to basic principles of law and gospel. He confesses his own sin (verse 176) but also his eager expectation of God's salvation.

Though he loves and cherishes the Word, he never loses sight of the purpose of the Word. It is not an end in itself, like just another great piece of literature. Its purpose is to put us into contact with the living God. It shows us that our sins have made us guilty before him. It shows us that he has removed the guilt of our sins. It changes our hearts so that we love him and begin to serve him gladly. We have come into fellowship with our Savior-God through the Word.

Through the Word we are equipped and strengthened for our life with him. For all these reasons we can say: "Oh, how I love your Word. It is sweeter than honey to my mouth. My lips overflow with praise, for you teach me your Word."

As a review of the main thoughts of this psalm, compare some of the passages you marked with the basic themes listed in the introduction to the psalm.

## Psalms 120–134: The Songs of Ascents

This group of psalms has the heading "The Songs of Ascents," literally "The Songs of Goings Up." A number of explanations have been offered for this title. One suggestion is that these psalms were sung when the priests were going up the steps of the temple for the worship service. Another suggestion is that the title refers to the going up to Jerusalem for the pilgrim festivals or the going up to Jerusalem when the exiles returned from Babylon. To the present day, the Hebrew term for moving to Israel is still "going up."

These explanations need not be mutually exclusive, since there is often a difference between the original reason for the composition of a hymn and its ultimate use. Some of these hymns originated as personal meditations of David. Others very likely originated as festival hymns. The collection, as it

Israelite pilgrim going to Jerusalem

now stands in the book of Psalms, appears to be a group of hymns selected for use during the pilgrim festivals. Some of them were used in the temple worship; others were probably used outside the temple service. Such hymns concerning the ascent to Jerusalem would, of course, be especially meaningful at the time of the return to Jerusalem after the captivity in Babylon.

In many of these psalms, parallelism is less important than it is in other sections of Psalms. As mentioned previously, there is an ascending thought pattern in some of these psalms, which has sometimes been suggested as the source of the name "songs of ascents." In this style successive verses pick up and develop a word from the preceding verse.

The songs of ascents are a carefully arranged selection of songs. There appear to be two groups of seven psalms arranged chiastically, that is, the 1st psalm matches up with the 14th, the 2nd with the 13th, and so on. The 15th psalm then serves as a benediction to the whole group. The matchups are as follows:

In Psalm 120 the pilgrim begins his journey surrounded by enemies in a distant land; in Psalm 133 he completes the journey amidst the pleasant unity of brothers.

Psalms 121 and 132 both speak of the help of the Lord, who establishes his people.

Psalm 122 speaks of the peace of Jerusalem; Psalm 131 speaks of the quiet rest of a child with its mother.

Psalms 123 and 130 both speak of the lowliness of the pilgrim.

Psalms 124 and 129 both speak of the Lord's help against oppressors.

Psalms 125 and 128 are both "Peace on Israel" psalms.

Psalms 126 and 127 both point to the rebuilding of the nation after captivity. Very often in biblical literature, the key point of the literary work is placed in the middle.

Although a few of the matchups, particularly the second and third, are not as precise as the others, the overall pattern seems too conspicuous to be merely coincidence.

# Psalm 120

## *A man of peace*

Psalm 120 is a logical introduction to the songs of ascents because it describes the distress of the psalmist when he is away from Jerusalem, the city of peace.

**A song of ascents.**

¹ I call on the LORD in my distress,
  and he answers me.
² Save me, O LORD, from lying lips
  and from deceitful tongues.

³ What will he do to you,
  and what more besides, O deceitful tongue?
⁴ He will punish you with a warrior's sharp arrows,
  with burning coals of the broom tree.

⁵ Woe to me that I dwell in Meshech,
  that I live among the tents of Kedar!
⁶ Too long have I lived among those who hate peace.

⁷ I am a man of peace;
  but when I speak,
    they are for war.

The psalmist turns first to the Lord to ask for help against the lying lips of his enemies. He then turns to his enemies to warn them of the punishment that awaits them if they persist in their ways. He says that he is exiled among barbarous people. Since Meshech is in present-day Turkey (far to the north) and Kedar is in Arabia (to the southeast), there is little likelihood the psalmist would have been exiled in both places. The terms, therefore, are probably used as figurative expressions for the psalmist's enemies closer to home. These terms represent the whole unbelieving world, which was hostile to Israel. Thus the psalm is generalized, so that it applies beyond the psalmist's personal experience.

Like the psalmist, the pilgrims who sing this psalm express their longing for the peace and harmony that exist among God's people in his courts. God's people cannot have peace when they live among God's enemies, since their two ways of life are incompatible (2 Corinthians 6:14-18). They can find peace only in their fellowship with the Lord and his people.

# Psalm 121

## *Help from the Lord*

Psalm 121 is a natural successor to Psalm 120. It speaks of the pilgrim's help in all adversity. Notice the ascending, steplike structure formed by the repetition of the words "help," "slumber," and "watch."

A song of ascents.

¹ I lift up my eyes to the hills—
where does my help come from?
² My help comes from the LORD,
the Maker of heaven and earth.

³ He will not let your foot slip—
he who watches over you will not slumber;

⁴indeed, he who watches over Israel
     will neither slumber nor sleep.
⁵The LORD watches over you—
  the LORD is your shade at your right hand;
⁶the sun will not harm you by day,
  nor the moon by night.
⁷The LORD will keep you from all harm—
  he will watch over your life;
⁸the LORD will watch over your coming
     and going both now and forevermore.

The opening line has an element of suspense in it. Hills and mountains are often dangerous places, the homes of wild animals and robbers. But hills and mountains are also a symbol of strength and security; we often speak of mountain strongholds. Line 1 is thus ambiguous—is the psalmist looking at the hills as a source of danger or as a source of help? Is his tone fearful or confident? The following lines resolve the ambiguity. The psalmist lifts up his eyes to the hills surrounding Jerusalem, the Holy City. However, his help and security do not come from the hills but from the Lord, who made the hills and everything else in the universe.

The rest of the psalm is an ascending promise of help. Each verse adds to the blessing. The Lord keeps the pilgrim safe from every type of danger in every time. The Lord is not a god who is on duty only at certain times. He is the untiring God, who is watching over his people at all times. He will keep the pilgrims safe both as they come to Jerusalem and as they leave it again. But the terms "coming in" and "going out" cover more than a journey to Jerusalem. They include the whole pilgrimage of life, from beginning to end.

Christians today use both the narrow and wide applications of these terms. In its narrow application, this psalm is an excellent prayer for travelers. In the wide application, we use verse 8 in the traditional Baptism liturgy as an expression of the Lord's care for the newly baptized child throughout its life. The Lord will watch our coming and our going now and forever.

# Psalm 122

### *The peace of Jerusalem*

Psalm 122 describes the pilgrim's destination, God's holy city of Jerusalem. Note the ascending pattern formed by such words as "tribes," "thrones," and "peace."

**A song of ascents. Of David.**

¹ **I rejoiced with those who said to me,**
 **"Let us go to the house of the LORD."**

² **Our feet are standing in your gates, O Jerusalem.**
³ **Jerusalem is built like a city**
 **that is closely compacted together.**
⁴ **That is where the tribes go up,**
 **the tribes of the LORD,**
 **to praise the name of the LORD**
 **according to the statute given to Israel.**
⁵ **There the thrones for judgment stand,**
 **the thrones of the house of David.**

⁶ **Pray for the peace of Jerusalem:**
 **"May those who love you be secure.**
⁷ **May there be peace within your walls**
 **and security within your citadels."**

⁸ **For the sake of my brothers and friends,**
 **I will say, "Peace be within you."**
⁹ **For the sake of the house of the LORD our God,**
 **I will seek your prosperity.**

This psalm contains two main elements: joy in the beauty of Jerusalem and a prayer for its blessing. The beauty of Jerusalem derived not so much from its construction as from the events that took place in it. In this city the Lord was worshiped in accordance with his will. In this city the judgments of God were received from his appointed rulers. All who loved God and his people therefore prayed for this city and its citizens.

However, like the other psalms about Jerusalem, this psalm points beyond the earthly city in the land of Israel. That city was glorious for the things God accomplished there, but it did not remain a city of peace, because it rejected the One who was its peace (Luke 19:42). Today strife and hatred rule there.

More glorious than Jerusalem is the spiritual Jerusalem, the church of all who believe. Each time we worship together, we are gathering in Jerusalem. This gathering will reach its most glorious stages in the new Jerusalem described in Revelation chapter 21. There God's people will live in complete safety. There David's greater Son will rule them with justice forever. This city is our joy. For this city our prayers ascend. To this city we are journeying.

# Psalm 123

## *The eyes of a servant*

In Psalm 123 the psalmist's eyes rise from Jerusalem to the Lord, who is enthroned in heaven. Notice the rising pattern in the words "eyes" and "mercy."

**A song of ascents.**

**¹I lift up my eyes to you,
  to you whose throne is in heaven.**

² As the eyes of slaves look
    to the hand of their master,
as the eyes of a maid look
    to the hand of her mistress,
so our eyes look to the LORD our God,
till he shows us his mercy.

³ Have mercy on us, O LORD,
have mercy on us,
for we have endured much contempt.
⁴ We have endured much ridicule from the proud,
much contempt from the arrogant.

Old Testament believers recognized that the hills were not their security and that Jerusalem itself was not their greatest joy. They looked to the Lord as their source of joy and as their fortress. As slaves depend on their masters for everything, so believers depend on the Lord for everything.

This psalm turns our attention to the scorn the pilgrim receives from those who surround him. The Jews' religious practices, which set them apart from the gentile world, did not win them much favor in the ancient world. On the contrary, pagans heaped ridicule upon them. Today things are no different for Christians, who take God at his word. They will receive scorn from every direction—from scoffers outside the church and from negative critics within, from scientists and sensualists, from lovers of wisdom and lovers of pleasure.

In Scripture the contrast between the humble and the proud is synonymous with the contrast between believers and unbelievers. The humble place God's wisdom ahead of the world's. They place God's honor ahead of their own. They look to him for vindication and wait patiently for his mercy, remembering that Christ bore the contempt of the world for us and that it is an honor to suffer for his name.

# Psalm 124

### *The Lord on our side*

Like Psalm 115, Psalm 124 gives all glory to God for Israel's safety in the land. In David's life the enemies could be either the followers of Saul or the followers of Absalom. However, since the tone of the psalm is more national than personal, some commentators identify the enemy as the Philistines, who were such a threat early in David's rule. Later in Israel's history, the psalm would have been applied to the nations who captured Israel and to the Samaritans who opposed Ezra and Nehemiah. Today we can apply it to all attacks against the church and its members.

Note the rapidly ascending pattern to peak danger and sudden resolution. Notice that verse 8 echoes Psalm 121.

**A song of ascents. Of David.**

¹ If the Lᴏʀᴅ had not been on our side—
let Israel say—
² if the Lᴏʀᴅ had not been on our side
when men attacked us,
³ when their anger flared against us,
they would have swallowed us alive;
⁴ the flood would have engulfed us,
the torrent would have swept over us,
⁵ the raging waters would have swept us away.

⁶ Praise be to the Lᴏʀᴅ,
who has not let us be torn by their teeth.
⁷ We have escaped like a bird
out of the fowler's snare;
the snare has been broken,
and we have escaped.

⁸ Our help is in the name of the Lᴏʀᴅ,
the Maker of heaven and earth.

The oppression of Israel is compared to a flood, a trap, and an attack by a wild animal. All of these are common pictures for the attacks of vicious enemies in the psalms. This psalm is general enough to apply to almost any experience of oppression by groups of Israelites or by the whole nation.

# Psalm 125

## *Mount Zion cannot be shaken*

One way in which God provides security for his people is by giving them good leaders.

A song of ascents.

¹Those who trust in the Lᴏʀᴅ are like Mount Zion,
  which cannot be shaken but endures forever.
²As the mountains surround Jerusalem,
  so the Lᴏʀᴅ surrounds his people
  both now and forevermore.

³The scepter of the wicked will not remain
      over the land allotted to the righteous,
  for then the righteous might use their hands
      to do evil.

⁴Do good, O Lᴏʀᴅ, to those who are good,
  to those who are upright in heart.
⁵But those who turn to crooked ways
  the Lᴏʀᴅ will banish with the evildoers.

  Peace be upon Israel.

The first section provides a general statement of the Lord's protection of his people. It does so by elaborating upon the reference to the mountains in Psalm 121. The mountains do contribute to the security of Jerusalem, but more important is the protective power of the Lord, which surrounds his people wherever they may be.

The remainder of the psalm speaks of one means by which the Lord provides security for his people: he gives them good leaders. A people often rise or fall to the level of their leaders. When Israel had corrupt leaders, the people became more corrupt. When they had leaders like David, Hezekiah, Josiah, Ezra, and Nehemiah, they were strengthened in their devotion to the Lord.

The Lord promises to remove the wicked leaders, who mislead his people. In the fullest sense, this was fulfilled when Christ came to assume the throne of David and to be the Great High Priest. It continues to be fulfilled in a secondary way when God provides good leaders to the church.

We should pray that the Lord will continue to provide us with leaders who are sound both in doctrine and in their way of life. Both the church and the nation need leaders who will oppose evil and support good. We should support, encourage, and defend such leaders. We should choose such leaders when we have a voice in the matter.

But the final resolution of the matter rests with the Lord. In the end he will call to account all corrupt rulers who have abused his trust. They will be cast out of God's kingdom so that God's people may live in peace under the King whom the Lord has provided for them.

# Psalm 126

### *The return of the captives*

Psalm 126 reaches the pinnacle of the Old Testament pilgrim's experience: the return to Jerusalem by the people of Israel who had been captives among the nations.

Notice the intricate interlocked parallelism of the last two verses. The parallels are indicated by the indentation below.

**A song of ascents.**

¹**When the Lord brought back the captives to Zion,\***
**we were like men who dreamed.**
²**Our mouths were filled with laughter,**
**our tongues with songs of joy.**
**Then it was said among the nations,**
**"The Lord has done great things for them."**
³**The Lord has done great things for us,**
**and we are filled with joy.**

⁴**Restore our fortunes, O Lord,**
**like streams in the Negev.**

⁵**Those who sow in tears**
**will reap with songs of joy.**
⁶**He who goes out weeping,**
**carrying seed to sow,**
**will return with songs of joy,**
**carrying sheaves with him.**

As translated in the main text, verse 1 suggests that this psalm may have originated as a celebration of the return of the captives from Babylon. But as the footnote indicates, the verse may be translated as a more general reference to the Lord's restoration of Zion's fortunes. When a similar phrase occurs in a psalm of David (Psalm 14:7), the NIV adopts the more general translation.

---

*NIV alternate: When the Lord restored the fortunes of Zion

Regardless of whether the more specific translation, "captives," or the more general reading, "fortunes," is followed in verse 1, the main application of Psalm 126 as one of the songs of ascents is to the return from Babylon. Nevertheless, the psalm is general enough to include every deliverance experienced by God's people, including the final delivery into eternal life.

The psalm consists of three main parts. The first section is an emotional outburst expressing the intense excitement and joy of God's people when he has restored their fortunes. Even their adversaries acknowledge the greatness of the Lord's deeds on their behalf.

The middle of the psalm is a prayer that the Lord will continue the restoration of the nation. After the return from Babylon, there was still a struggle, and a lot of hard work remained to rebuild the nation, the city, and the temple.

The picture used to illustrate the sudden restoration of the nation is the coming of the winter rains to the dry Negev in southern Israel. During the hot, rainless summer, the streams are empty and the land is desolate. The swelling of the streams from the winter rains restores the beautiful flowers of spring to the land. The picture is of sudden restoration, accomplished without human planning or initiative. Judah was restored suddenly when God raised up Cyrus of Persia and moved him to decree the return.

The picture is quite different in the third section of the psalm. Here the long, hard toil of the farmer between planting and harvest is the point of comparison. Before the harvest is gathered, before the restoration is complete, there is a lot of work to be done by the Lord's coworkers. They must toil in the fields in the heat of the day, with the sweat of their brow before the harvest can finally be gathered in.

If we apply these illustrations to our own experience of God's restoration of our fortunes, we see that they picture both our sudden, effortless release from captivity and our joining in the work of harvest, which follows. The Lord has released us from sin by a restoration that is as sudden, as effortless, and as exciting as the blooming of the desert in spring. He did this when he brought us to faith in Christ. Through him we have complete forgiveness of sins. In this sense our restoration is complete.

But in another sense, there is much to do before our fortunes are restored. We are not yet a finished product. We continue the bitter struggle against sin, which produces tears and sorrow. We toil to relieve those who suffer from the effects of sin all around us. We labor to plant and tend the seed of the Word so that the harvest on the Last Day will be abundant. God has not promised that the work will be easy. We will experience ingratitude and opposition. But we do have the promise that if we do not grow weary, we will experience a harvest at the appropriate time (2 Corinthians 15:58).

# Psalm 127

## *The Lord builds the house*

Psalm 127 elaborates on the relationship between human labor and divine blessing that was introduced in the preceding psalm.

**A song of ascents. Of Solomon.**

¹ **Unless the Lord builds the house,**
**its builders labor in vain.**
**Unless the Lord watches over the city,**
**the watchmen stand guard in vain.**

² **In vain you rise early and stay up late,**
**toiling for food to eat—**
**for he grants sleep to those he loves.**

³ Sons are a heritage from the LORD,
 children a reward from him.
⁴ Like arrows in the hands of a warrior
   are sons born in one's youth.
⁵ Blessed is the man whose quiver is full of them.
 They will not be put to shame
 when they contend with their enemies in the gate.

"The house" in verse 1 is an ambiguous term. It is a very common term for the temple in Jerusalem. This would be a very meaningful reference both in the time of Solomon and in the later use of this psalm, when the temple was being rebuilt after the exile. "House" could also be a generic term, referring to any human building project or endeavor. "House" also means "family" in biblical usage, and this connotation of the word is picked up in the last part of the psalm.

The work of watching over the city was especially important during the rebuilding of Jerusalem's walls during the time of Nehemiah. Because of the threat of a surprise attack by the Samaritans, the builders had to work with tools in one hand and weapons in the other. Thus the workers and the watchers were one.

Both of these pictures elaborate on the interrelationship of divine blessing and human work. No human effort can prosper without God's blessing, but in earthly matters human effort is necessary. Builders are to build. Watchmen are to watch. Workers are to work. Farmers are to farm. All of them are to put forth their best effort. But then they are to relax, trust the Lord, and be content with what he has provided for them. Worry and discontent will only diminish their enjoyment of God's blessings.

The abrupt change of subject matter to children is really quite natural, since the focus of these psalms is on possession of the land. The promise of the land and the promise of the seed belong together. There could be no building up of the nation without children who would carry on the work and keep the promise of the Savior alive. The emphasis on sound family life became especially important during the days of Ezra and Nehemiah, when many, even among the leaders of Israel, were deserting their first marriages and intermarrying with their heathen neighbors. Personal satisfaction had become a more important goal than raising a godly family. Our society is repeating that mistake.

Children are a blessing of the Lord. This message needs to be proclaimed strongly in our day, when self-fulfillment and materialism seem to have drastically changed people's attitudes toward children. The prevalence of abortion, child abuse, child neglect, and divorce stand as a terrible indictment of our society and its values. In God's view passing on the heritage of faith is the most important goal of each generation. It is doubtful if many in our society, including many in the church, would list this as the first priority of life.

Many of God's gifts are also responsibilities. God's Word is one such gift. Children are another. Children will be a blessing in the long run; in this psalm they defend their father against his foes. But for many years they are, in one sense, a liability. Before they can contribute, they must receive. But this investment in children is the best investment in the future, both for the church and for society.

This psalm, which speaks of contentment at work and contentment at home, addresses two of the most urgent needs of our society. It gives us a message to apply in our own lives and to share with our society. It was tragic that Solomon did not practice more fully in his own life the truth he advocates in this psalm. As the book of Ecclesiastes points out, Solomon had to learn the hard way. It will also be tragic for our society if we fail to learn the lessons taught by this psalm. We too will learn the hard way.

# Psalm 128

## *A blessed family*

Psalm 128 repeats the theme of the preceding psalm: a contented enjoyment of the possessions and the family, which the Lord gives, is true happiness. This psalm is both a promise of blessing and a prayer of blessing.

**A song of ascents.**

*Promise*

> ¹ **Blessed are all who fear the LORD,**
> **who walk in his ways.**
>
> ² **You will eat the fruit of your labor;**
> **blessings and prosperity will be yours.**
>
> ³ **Your wife will be like a fruitful vine**
> **within your house;**
> **your sons will be like olive shoots**
> **around your table.**
>
> ⁴ **Thus is the man blessed who fears the LORD.**

*Prayer*

> ⁵ **May the LORD bless you from Zion**
> **all the days of your life;**
> **may you see the prosperity of Jerusalem,**
> ⁶ **and may you live to see your children's children.**
>
> **Peace be upon Israel.**

This psalm, which is a blessing on the family, is also a blessing on the nation, because as the family goes, so goes the nation. The blessing of a nation starts with godliness in the hearts of parents. Such parents fear God and obey his commandments. Their strength flows to the children through the contentment and peace it produces in the family.

From solid families strength flows to the nation. From solid, godly families come workers who will build up the nation, parents who will raise godly children, and children who are our hope for the future. Without such families the future is dark. From such families the nation and the church will find strength.

# Psalm 129

## *No blessing*

Psalm 129 contrasts with Psalm 128, which speaks of the blessing of the godly. The ungodly, who oppress the godly, will experience no blessing.

A song of ascents.

¹They have greatly oppressed me from my youth—
let Israel say—
²they have greatly oppressed me from my youth,
but they have not gained the victory over me.
³Plowmen have plowed my back
and made their furrows long.

⁴But the LORD is righteous;
he has cut me free from the cords of the wicked.

⁵May all who hate Zion be turned back in shame.
⁶May they be like grass on the roof,
which withers before it can grow;

⁷**with it the reaper cannot fill his hands,**
  **nor the one who gathers fill his arms.**
⁸**May those who pass by not say,**
    **"The blessing of the L**ORD** be upon you;**
    **we bless you in the name of the L**ORD**."**

The description of the oppressors is general enough to apply to any situation in Israel's history. It fits the Egyptians, who persecuted Israel in the early days. The description would also fit the Assyrians and Babylonians, who carried Israel and Judah into captivity. In the post-exilic period, the main oppressors of Israel were Sanballat the Samaritan and Tobiah the Ammonite. A similar description of Christ's oppressors occurs in Isaiah 50:6. Plowing is a graphic picture for the whip marks inflicted on the backs of the persecuted.

Whoever they may be, in whatever time of history they may exist, the oppressors of God's people will be uprooted. In Psalm 128 the righteous are compared to fruitful trees and productive vines, but the ungodly are uprooted weeds, which shrivel up and have no value.

# Psalm 130

### *Out of the depths*

Psalm 130 is classified as one of the seven penitential psalms. The psalm begins with a personal confession but takes on a congregational tone at the end. It is especially the congregational aspect that makes it appropriate for the festivals and for times of national repentance like those that occurred under the leadership of Ezra.

A song of ascents.

¹**Out of the depths I cry to you, O** LORD;
²**O Lord, hear my voice.**
 **Let your ears be attentive to my cry for mercy.**

³ **If you, O** LORD, **kept a record of sins,**
 **O Lord, who could stand?**
⁴**But with you there is forgiveness;**
 **therefore you are feared.**

⁵**I wait for the** LORD, **my soul waits,**
 **and in his word I put my hope.**
⁶**My soul waits for the Lord**
 **more than watchmen wait for the morning,**
 **more than watchmen wait for the morning.**

⁷**O Israel, put your hope in the** LORD,
 **for with the** LORD **is unfailing love**
 **and with him is full redemption.**
⁸ **He himself will redeem Israel from all their sins.**

The psalm falls naturally into four parts. In the opening plea, the psalmist cries out for mercy. The "depths" from which he calls could be the depths of trouble and adversity, but since there is no other reference to sickness or persecution in the psalm, it seems best to regard the depths as the depths of sin. The psalmist realizes that his sin has separated him from God. His guilt has plunged him into sorrow and despair. He knows that self-help and positive thinking will not pull him out of the depths.

But he does not remain in the depths. He knows that the Lord is a forgiving God. God has perfect knowledge of our sins, but he does not charge them against us, because Christ

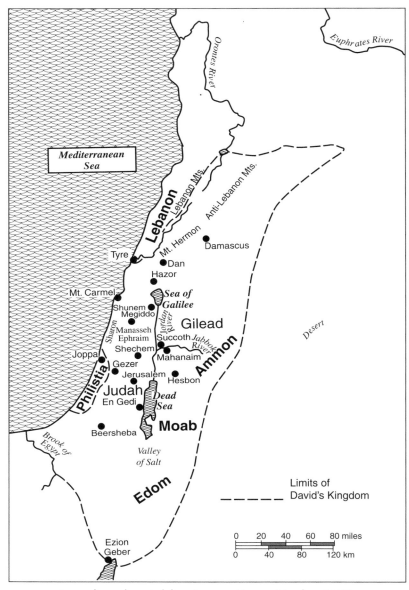

Israel and neighboring nations (Psalm 108)

paid for them. "God was reconciling the world to himself in Christ, not counting men's sins against them" (2 Corinthians 5:19). With Christ as our defender, we will successfully pass God's judgment and stand safely in his presence. The "fear" that flows from forgiveness is not dread and terror but reverence, love, and honor for the God who has forgiven us.

The psalmist waits eagerly for the day when he will fully experience forgiveness in the presence of God. He looks for the Lord's promised coming as eagerly as a night watchman looks for the light of dawn, which tells him that his long night of labor is almost over.

In the conclusion the psalmist looks beyond himself to the whole people of Israel. He invites them to join him in his confession and in his confidence. They can be sure that God will provide complete payment for their sins. He will forgive them fully and freely. He will free them from all the effects of their sins. When this is done, they will live not in the depths but on the heights of glory with the Lord.

# Psalm 131

## *My heart is not proud*

The statement of humility in Psalm 131 is an appropriate follow-up to the confession of Psalm 130.

**A song of ascents. Of David.**

¹**My heart is not proud, O LORD,**
 **my eyes are not haughty;**
 **I do not concern myself with great matters**
 **or things too wonderful for me.**
²**But I have stilled and quieted my soul;**
 **like a weaned child with its mother,**
 **like a weaned child is my soul within me.**

**³O Israel, put your hope in the L<small>ORD</small>**
**both now and forevermore.**

The humility expressed in verse 1 is not false humility, which refuses God's calling as Moses did. It is not a lack of confidence, which leads a person to idle his life away. It is not negligence of the duties God has given us. It is, rather, the recognition that some works remain in God's sphere, not ours. We cannot pay for a single sin by heaping up zealous works or by burdening ourselves with self-punishment. We rest in peace, confident of God's forgiveness. We cannot convert a single soul by pressuring and manipulating. We only plant the seed and leave the rest to the Holy Spirit. By worrying we cannot add an hour to our lives. We leave our lives in God's hands.

Instead of fretting and striving over things that are beyond our ability and beyond our control, we should rest quietly, like a young child with his mother. This child is no longer a baby, howling for milk, demanding satisfaction the instant he feels a craving. He is a child no longer nursing, a child who has learned to trust his mother to provide, who waits quietly for his needs to be fulfilled. God's people are still children who depend on their Father's care and provision, but they are not spiritual babies who demand satisfaction according to their timetable. Like respectful, trusting children, they wait on the Lord.

# Psalm 132

## *Remember David*

Psalm 132 connects the songs of ascents with the messianic promise. The songs of ascents focus on the temple in Jerusalem. David had promised to build this house for

God, but in 2 Samuel chapter 7, Nathan the prophet informed David that he would not be able to build a house for the Lord, but the Lord would build a house for him.

David's son Solomon would build the temple, the house of the Lord, but through Jesus Christ, a later descendant of David, the Lord would build a greater house of David, namely, the kingdom of Christ, the church. The two main parts of the psalm are based on David's promise to the Lord and the Lord's greater promise to David.

**A song of ascents.**

*David's oath*

¹**O Lord, remember David**
**and all the hardships he endured.**
²**He swore an oath to the Lord**
**and made a vow to the Mighty One of Jacob:**
        ³**"I will not enter my house or go to my bed—**
        ⁴**I will allow no sleep to my eyes,**
        **no slumber to my eyelids,**
        ⁵**till I find a place for the Lord,**
        **a dwelling for the Mighty One of Jacob."**

A priority of David's reign was to establish a home for the ark of the covenant, which had not had an appropriate home since the tabernacle at Shiloh had been destroyed. David was able to undertake this project only after overcoming many years of hardships. The hardships mentioned in verse 1 may include not only David's suffering at the hands of Saul and other enemies, but also the setback he suffered when he tried to move the ark to Jerusalem without following proper procedures (2 Samuel 6).

Furthermore, after David had defeated his enemies and secured the peace and safety of his kingdom, he promised to build a temple for the Lord because he did not think that it was right for the Lord's ark to be in a tent while David had a fine palace.

At first the prophet Nathan encouraged this project, but then the Lord revealed that it would be David's son who would complete the project. Though David could not finish the project himself, he made preparations for the building with the encouragement and support of the people of Israel.

### Israel's response

⁶**We heard it in Ephrathah,**
**we came upon it in the fields of Jaar:**
⁷**"Let us go to his dwelling place;**
**let us worship at his footstool—**
⁸**arise, O LORD, and come to your resting place,**
**you and the ark of your might.**
⁹**May your priests be clothed with righteousness;**
**may your saints sing for joy.**
¹⁰**For the sake of David your servant,**
**do not reject your anointed one."**

These verses are the people's endorsement of the temple project. The establishment of the temple in Jerusalem was a three-step process: David brought the ark of the covenant to Jerusalem, David made preparations for the building, and finally Solomon built and dedicated the temple. The people of Israel joined in all three phases of the project.

The people describe the invitation to participate as coming from Ephrathah, another name for David's hometown of Bethlehem, and from Jaar, another name for Kiriath Jearim, the city where the ark was kept until David brought it to Jerusalem. This twofold invitation stresses David's personal concern and the importance of the presence of the Lord, symbolized by the ark. (Another possibility is that the regional name Ephrathah includes Kiriath Jearim as well as Bethlehem, and that here it is synonymous with Jaar.)

Verses 8 and 9 are based on the lines that were recited whenever the ark was moved during the wilderness years (Numbers 10:35). Solomon used these words and a verse very similar to verse 10 at the time the temple was dedicated. The text of the NIV separates verse 10 from the people's statement in verses 8 and 9 by its placement of the quotation marks, but in the text of this commentary, the punctuation of verse 10 has been changed to connect it with verses 8 and 9, as it is in 2 Chronicles 6:41,42.

## The Lord's oath

11 The LORD swore an oath to David,
a sure oath that he will not revoke:
"One of your own descendants
I will place on your throne—
12 if your sons keep my covenant
and the statutes I teach them,
then their sons will sit on your
throne for ever and ever."

13 For the LORD has chosen Zion,
he has desired it for his dwelling:

14 "This is my resting place for ever and ever;
here I will sit enthroned,
for I have desired it—
15 I will bless her with abundant provisions;
her poor will I satisfy with food.
16 I will clothe her priests with salvation,
and her saints will ever sing for joy.
17 Here I will make a horn grow for David
and set up a lamp for my anointed one.
18 I will clothe his enemies with shame,
but the crown on his head will be resplendent."

In 2 Samuel chapter 7, the Lord promised David that he would have a descendant who would rule from his throne forever. This promise is also the focus of such psalms as Psalms 72 and 89.

This promise was fulfilled in a preliminary way when the Lord preserved David's dynasty on the throne of Judah in spite of the upheaval that characterized the northern kingdom of Israel. However, many of the kings of Judah were not godly rulers. Because of their poor leadership, the temple built by Solomon was finally destroyed, and the nation went into captivity. The rule of the Davidic dynasty over the land of Israel ended.

Nevertheless, the royal line of David was preserved until Jesus was born as the son of Mary and the heir of Joseph. Jesus was the Son of David who fulfilled the promise of an eternal kingdom. He provides peace and justice to the Israel of faith, and he builds God's true Israel, the church of all believers. Entering into his glorious kingdom is the goal of every pilgrim on this earth.

# Psalm 133

## *Pleasant unity*

Psalm 133, another song of ascents, celebrates the true unity and fellowship of God's people, who gather in his presence.

**A song of ascents. Of David.**

¹**How good and pleasant it is**
**when brothers live together in unity!**
²**It is like precious oil poured on the head,**
**running down on the beard,**
**running down on Aaron's beard,**
**down upon the collar of his robes.**

³**It is as if the dew of Hermon were falling
    on Mount Zion.
For there the** L**ORD** **bestows his blessing,
even life forevermore.**

The unity of God's people is an occasion for joy. Anointing with oil was a symbol of joyful celebration and rich blessing from God. Like anointing oil, fellowship with God flows down and spreads out to all who receive him. The unity of God's people is as refreshing and invigorating as abundant dew in a dry climate. Although Mount Zion is much lower than Mount Hermon, it is more richly blessed, because it is the place of the Lord's presence.

This pleasant unity of God's people is not mere organizational unity. It is not a unity based on political compromise. It is a unity based on shared loyalty to God and his Word. God-pleasing unity is not merely working together; it is working together for the truth. True unity, which will be a blessing to us and to others, is not based on silent acceptance of false teaching or evil conduct. It is based on agreement in the truth. Such agreement includes brotherly correction of those who err. Such unity is indeed a joy and a blessing.

# Psalm 134

## *The pilgrim's blessing*

Psalm 134 is a closing benediction to the songs of ascents. The first two verses are clearly the admonition of the people to the priests and Levites to be faithful in their ministry. Verse 3 may be the priests' response to the people.

**A song of ascents.**

*The people*

> ¹Praise the LORD, all you servants of the LORD
> who minister by night in the house of the LORD.
> ²Lift up your hands in the sanctuary
> and praise the LORD.

*The priests*

> ³May the LORD, the Maker of heaven and earth,
> bless you from Zion.

This benediction brings this collection of psalms to a fitting conclusion. Zion, the place of God's presence, is the source of all blessing. Since the Lord is the maker of heaven and earth, he can provide every blessing for his people.

# Psalms 135–137

Psalms 135 to 137 are not songs of ascents, but they are closely related to them in theme.

# Psalm 135

### *Israel, praise the Lord*

Psalm 135 could be called a composite psalm or review psalm, since it picks up themes from several other psalms. Every one of its verses has a parallel somewhere else in Scripture. Its strongest connections are with Psalms 113 to 118, the Passover hallel. Its opening and closing hallelujah (praise the Lord) connect it with the hallel. It also echoes parts of Psalms 115 and 118.

Psalm 135 is also a connecting psalm. Its opening line echoes Psalm 134, the conclusion of the songs of ascents. Its emphasis on creation and the exodus points ahead to Psalm 136. It apparently was designed to be a liturgical psalm that covers key themes of worship. The blessings that the Lord has showered on his chosen people Israel are the main concern of this psalm.

### Introduction

> ¹ **Praise the Lord.**
>
> **Praise the name of the Lord;**
> **praise him, you servants of the Lord,**
> ² **you who minister in the house of the Lord,**
> **in the courts of the house of our God.**
> ³ **Praise the Lord, for the Lord is good;**
> **sing praise to his name, for that is pleasant.**
>
> ⁴ **For the Lord has chosen Jacob to be his own,**
> **Israel to be his treasured possession.**

The introduction indicates that this psalm was associated with temple worship. The priests and Levites are invited to praise God for his goodness to Israel. They are to rejoice in the blessings God has showered on Israel. These blessings are described in the next section of the psalm.

### The superiority of the Lord

> ⁵ **I know that the Lord is great,**
> **that our Lord is greater than all gods.**
> ⁶ **The Lord does whatever pleases him,**
> **in the heavens and on the earth,**
> **in the seas and all their depths.**

⁷He makes clouds rise from the ends of the earth;
   he sends lightning with the rain
   and brings out the wind from his storehouses.

⁸ He struck down the firstborn of Egypt,
   the firstborn of men and animals.
⁹He sent his signs and wonders into your midst,
         O Egypt,
   against Pharaoh and all his servants.
¹⁰He struck down many nations
         and killed mighty kings—
¹¹Sihon king of the Amorites,
   Og king of Bashan and all the kings of Canaan—
¹²and he gave their land as an inheritance,
   an inheritance to his people Israel.

¹³ Your name, O LORD, endures forever,
   your renown, O LORD, through all generations.
¹⁴For the LORD will vindicate his people
   and have compassion on his servants.

¹⁵ The idols of the nations are silver and gold,
   made by the hands of men.
¹⁶They have mouths, but cannot speak,
   eyes, but they cannot see;
¹⁷they have ears, but cannot hear,
   nor is there breath in their mouths.
¹⁸Those who make them will be like them,
   and so will all who trust in them.

The section concerning the Lord's superiority over the imaginary gods of the nations reviews a portion of Psalm 115. Idols are do-nothings who can bring no blessing to those who serve them. The Lord, on the other hand, is active both in nature and in history. As Creator and preserver, he governs the world for the good of his people. He likewise directs the course of history for the ultimate good of his people. This work of the Lord for his people will be presented more fully in Psalm 136.

## Conclusion

<sup>19</sup>O house of Israel, praise the LORD;
   O house of Aaron, praise the LORD;
<sup>20</sup>O house of Levi, praise the LORD;
   you who fear him, praise the LORD.

<sup>21</sup> Praise be to the LORD from Zion,
   to him who dwells in Jerusalem.

Praise the LORD.

This conclusion connects Psalm 135 with both the Passover hallel and the songs of ascents. Both of these groups emphasize the blessing of the Promised Land for Israel. The people and their leaders find their greatest joy in the presence of the Lord in his temple.

# Psalm 136

## *His love endures forever*

The refrain repeated with every verse suggests that Psalm 136 was designed for antiphonal singing in the temple service. Very likely one choir sang the message line, and another choir responded with the refrain. The refrain, "His love endures forever," expresses the theme of the psalm. The word that the NIV translates "love" is not the general Hebrew word for *love*. It is a word that has the connotation of undeserved love and mercy, and it often refers to deeds of love and mercy that are a fulfillment of a covenant. The psalm summarizes the Lord's covenant faithfulness to his people and calls upon them to praise him for his loving deeds.

### Introduction

> [1] **Give thanks to the LORD, for he is good.**
>> *His love endures forever.*
> [2] **Give thanks to the God of gods.**
>> *His love endures forever.*
> [3] **Give thanks to the Lord of lords:**
>> *His love endures forever.*

This invitation to praise reminds us of the Lord's superiority over all imaginary gods, as proclaimed in Psalm 135. It invites Israel to praise the Lord for his unfailing goodness to Israel. The two most important demonstrations of God's goodness are proclaimed in the next two sections of the psalm.

### His creating love

> [4] **to him who alone does great wonders,**
>> *His love endures forever.*
> [5] **who by his understanding made the heavens,**
>> *His love endures forever.*
> [6] **who spread out the earth upon the waters,**
>> *His love endures forever.*
> [7] **who made the great lights—**
>> *His love endures forever.*
> [8] **the sun to govern the day,**
>> *His love endures forever.*
> [9] **the moon and stars to govern the night;**
>> *His love endures forever.*

The story of creation is a story of God's love. He made everything in the universe for the good of his people.

Although the whole human race rebelled against him, the Lord continues to provide sun and rain, food and life, for both the evil and the good. Although God gives daily bread even to the ungrateful, his people gladly acknowledge that the preservation of the earth and its blessings is a continued display of God's love. They are confident that if the Lord watches over every sparrow, he will continue to provide for his people.

## His redeeming love

<sup>10</sup>**to him who struck down the firstborn of Egypt**
*His love endures forever.*
<sup>11</sup>**and brought Israel out from among them**
*His love endures forever.*
<sup>12</sup>**with a mighty hand and outstretched arm;**
*His love endures forever.*
<sup>13</sup>**to him who divided the Red Sea asunder**
*His love endures forever.*
<sup>14</sup>**and brought Israel through the midst of it,**
*His love endures forever.*
<sup>15</sup>**but swept Pharaoh and his army into the Red Sea;**
*His love endures forever.*
<sup>16</sup>**to him who led his people through the desert,**
*His love endures forever.*
<sup>17</sup>**who struck down great kings,**
*His love endures forever.*
<sup>18</sup>**and killed mighty kings—**
*His love endures forever.*
<sup>19</sup>**Sihon king of the Amorites**
*His love endures forever.*
<sup>20</sup>**and Og king of Bashan—**
*His love endures forever.*
<sup>21</sup>**and gave their land as an inheritance,**
*His love endures forever.*
<sup>22</sup>**an inheritance to his servant Israel;**
*His love endures forever.*

The Lord redeemed his people from slavery in Egypt by the power he displayed in the plagues. He led them safely through the wilderness and gave them victory over Sihon and Og, kings east of the Jordan. He then gave them victory over the kings and peoples of Canaan, who were west of the Jordan. When the Lord had finished his work, Israel was secure in the land that had been promised to Abraham.

Similar reviews of history are found in Psalms 78, 105, and 106.

*His continuing love*
> <sup>23</sup>**to the One who remembered us in our low estate**
>> *His love endures forever.*
> <sup>24</sup>**and freed us from our enemies,**
>> *His love endures forever.*
> <sup>25</sup>**and who gives food to every creature.**
>> *His love endures forever.*
>
> <sup>26</sup> **Give thanks to the God of heaven.**
>> *His love endures forever.*

The conclusion of the psalm restates the Lord's redeeming and creating love in general terms. The redeeming love of the Lord reached its high point when Christ redeemed us from our enemies—sin, death, and Satan—and secured our eternal inheritance. He daily and richly provides all we need for body and life. For all this we too should sing: "Give thanks to the Lord, for he is good. His love endures forever."

# Psalm 137

## *By the rivers of Babylon*

Psalm 137 explicitly links these three transitional psalms and the songs of ascents to the celebration of the return from

Babylon. Like Psalm 120, which began this entire cycle, Psalm 137 looks at the dark side of the picture. Like Psalm 120, it refers to the harshness of the oppression against Israel. It contrasts the attitude of the oppressors with that of Israel. It responds to the cruelty of the enemy with one of the harshest curses in the psalms. Before reading it, you may want to review the general comments on the imprecatory psalms in the introduction in Volume 1.

> ¹ **By the rivers of Babylon**
> **we sat and wept when we remembered Zion.**
> ² **There on the poplars we hung our harps,**
> ³ **for there our captors asked us for songs,**
> **our tormentors demanded songs of joy;**
> **they said, "Sing us one of the songs of Zion!"**
>
> ⁴ **How can we sing the songs of the LORD**
> **while in a foreign land?**
> ⁵ **If I forget you, O Jerusalem,**
> **may my right hand forget ⌊its skill⌋ .**
> ⁶ **May my tongue cling to the roof of my mouth**
> **if I do not remember you,**
> **if I do not consider Jerusalem my highest joy.**
>
> ⁷ **Remember, O LORD, what the Edomites did**
> **on the day Jerusalem fell.**
> **"Tear it down," they cried,**
> **"tear it down to its foundations!"**
> ⁸ **O Daughter of Babylon, doomed to destruction,**
> **happy is he who repays you**
> **for what you have done to us—**
> ⁹ **he who seizes your infants**
> **and dashes them against the rocks.**

This psalm is a sad counterpart to the many psalms that speak of the joy Israel experienced during the festivals at

God's house in Jerusalem. If the ascent to Jerusalem was the pinnacle of joy, nothing could be worse than being torn away from the worship that took place in the house of the Lord.

The psalmist describes the grief of the exiles as they sat along the rivers and canals of Babylon and the surrounding territory. When the Babylonians asked them to perform the happy songs of Zion, it may have been done in tactless ignorance or in sarcastic mockery of Israel's faith. In either case the grief Israel suffered was just as intense, because the mere singing of the songs of Zion would remind the exiles of the joys they were missing by being torn away from Jerusalem.

Since the sacrifices that were the central part of Old Testament worship could be offered only in Jerusalem, the worship of Israel was not as portable as ours is. As long as the Old Testament sacrifices were valid, Israel was attached to Jerusalem in a way more profound than our attachment to any one place. Only in Jerusalem could the full worship prescribed by the Lord be offered. Only there could the happy songs of ascents be most meaningfully sung.

The psalmist would prefer to be rendered crippled or dumb rather than to use the songs of the Lord to entertain God's enemies. To him the psalms of Zion were not just great music and fine entertainment. They were sacred songs of worship reserved for the Lord.

King Belshazzar's profane misuse of the sacred vessels from the temple during his drinking party is another example of the scorn the Babylonians showed for the Lord and his worship (Daniel 5). In both cases something sacred to the Lord was being used for heathen entertainment. Such mockery showed that Israel's enemies were the Lord's enemies too.

Nevertheless, modern readers are shocked at the harshness of the curses that conclude this psalm. Two peoples fall under this curse. The Edomites are singled out because as descendants of Esau, Jacob's brother, they should have been Israel's closest associates. Israel had not tried to take away Edom's land at the time of the conquest, but Edom had refused Israel safe passage. They remained Israel's bitter enemies throughout the years. When Jerusalem fell, the Edomites helped the Babylonians and celebrated Israel's fall, since this gave them a chance to take over some of the land that the Lord had promised to Israel. In effect, they were trying to undo the promise to Jacob.

The Babylonians fall under God's curse because of their haughty attitude, their cruelty, and their mockery of the Lord's worship. Their ungodly arrogance is denounced and their doom is predicted in many of the prophetic books.

It is important to remember that the curses of Psalm 137 are not originally the psalmist's curses. They are the Lord's curses, which the psalmist has made his own. The destruction of Edom was the fulfillment of prophecy, particularly the prophecy of Obadiah.

In Isaiah 13:16, which was written about two hundred years before Babylon's fall, the destruction of Babylon was prophesied in almost the exact terms used in Psalm 137. The destruction of the children who were too young to be transported into slavery was a common practice in ancient warfare. Since this cruelty was apparently practiced by the Babylonians during their campaigns of conquest against Israel, Babylon would receive from its Persian and Medean conquerors the same treatment it had inflicted on Israel (Jeremiah 50:29; 51:56).

As horrible as the practices of ancient warfare were, present-day readers should not be too smug in dismissing such practices as relics of a prescientific, unenlightened age.

The horrors produced by sinful man are no less terrible in our era, when warring nations routinely bomb civilian populations from a distance.

The destructions of Edom and Babylon were both fore-shadowings of judgment day. As horrifying as they were, they are only a pale reflection of the horrors of the Last Day and of damnation. Psalm 137 is the strong medicine that our society needs to hear. Today people have lost an awareness of the horrifying consequences of unforgiven sin; the writer of Psalm 137 had not. He did not tone down his shocking message with a happy ending. There will be no happy ending for the impenitent enemies of God. We need to let the strong message of Psalm 137, shocking as it is, stand as an awesome warning of the severity of God's judgment against sin. Sugarcoating and watering down that message is not a kindness to a world that is complacent about sin.

# Psalms 138–145

This supplementary collection of Davidic psalms consists of six prayers bracketed by introductory and concluding psalms of praise. It is appropriate that the book of Psalms closes with a Davidic collection, since Psalms is preeminently David's book.

# Psalm 138

### *May the kings praise you*

Psalm 138 begins and ends with David's commitment to praise the Lord for the help and protection David has received from him. The middle section is the key to the special theme of the psalm. It calls upon all kings to join David in acknowledging the Lord.

As the first psalm of a group so often does, Psalm 138 forms a bridge between the preceding and following groups of psalms. Verse 8, "Your love . . . endures forever," looks back to Psalm 136 and the preceding group. Verse 6, "the Lord looks down and knows," looks ahead to the content of Psalm 139.

**Of David.**

¹I will praise you, O LORD, with all my heart;
before the "gods" I will sing your praise.
²I will bow down toward your holy temple
and will praise your name
for your love and your faithfulness,
for you have exalted above all things
your name and your word.
³When I called, you answered me;
you made me bold and stouthearted.

⁴May all the kings of the earth praise you,
O LORD, when they hear the words of your mouth.
⁵May they sing of the ways of the LORD,
for the glory of the LORD is great.

⁶Though the LORD is on high, he looks
upon the lowly,
but the proud he knows from afar.
⁷Though I walk in the midst of trouble,
you preserve my life;
you stretch out your hand
against the anger of my foes,
with your right hand you save me.
⁸The LORD will fulfill ⌊his purpose⌋ for me;
your love, O LORD, endures forever—
do not abandon the works of your hands.

The term "gods" may refer to heathen gods or, more rarely, to angels or even to earthly rulers. Since this psalm is David's invitation to the kings of the earth to join him in praising the true God, the rare meaning "earthly rulers" is appropriate here. The NIV's use of quotation marks around "gods" seems to indicate that the translators were adopting this interpretation of the term.

David supports his invitation by his testimony concerning the blessings the Lord has given to him. David briefly catalogs these blessings. The Lord's love and faithfulness are revealed in his promises and his actions. Nothing surpasses the greatness of the reputation God has established by his Word and his actions. David personally experienced this goodness of the Lord when the Lord rescued him from his enemies. The Lord gave David the boldness to carry out the mission the Lord entrusted to him. One of the ways the Lord helps us overcome adversity is by giving us the necessary courage and decisiveness to deal with it.

Verse 6 is transitional; it serves both as a warning to the kings not to scorn David's invitation to praise the Lord and as a comfort to David to continue to trust in the Lord. This twofold application also points ahead to Psalm 139.

Verse 8, "The LORD will fulfill his purpose for me," is a good statement to remember in every situation. The Lord fulfilled his purpose for David in spite of the intentions of Saul and Absalom and in spite of David's sins. All things, even adversity, worked for David's good. All things indeed work for the good of those who love God. Whatever life may bring, the Lord will fulfill his purpose for us.

# Psalm 139

## *God's attributes*

Psalm 139 is a practical discussion of God's attributes. In the Bible there is no abstract, philosophical discussion of God's nature and attributes. We always see God in action, working to uphold good and to oppose evil. Each of God's attributes serves as a comfort and as a warning: a warning to those who disobey God and a comfort to those who believe in him.

**For the director of music. Of David. A psalm.**

### *All-knowing*

¹O LORD, you have searched me
and you know me.
²You know when I sit and when I rise;
you perceive my thoughts from afar.
³You discern my going out and my lying down;
you are familiar with all my ways.
⁴Before a word is on my tongue
you know it completely, O LORD.

⁵You hem me in—behind and before;
you have laid your hand upon me.

⁶Such knowledge is too wonderful for me,
too lofty for me to attain.

God knows our every move, our every thought. He even knows what we will say and what we will do in the future. Such knowledge is incomprehensible to us who are limited by time and space. Such knowledge is threatening to sinners. We all would feel uncomfortable in the presence of someone who knew all our secrets. How much more uncomfortable it is for sinners to have all their actions, words, and thoughts known by the holy God!

But to those who are at peace with God through the forgiveness of sins, God's total knowledge is a comfort. God knows our weaknesses, not to take advantage of them but to help us overcome them. God knows our troubles, not to exploit them but to help us with them.

To be hemmed in by God's knowledge and to have his hand on us can be either a comfort or a threat. Our response depends on one crucial relationship: are we sinners trying to escape an angry judge, or are we dear children in the arms of a loving Father? It is faith that changes us from fearful sinners to confident children.

*Present everywhere*

> ⁷**Where can I go from your Spirit?**
> **Where can I flee from your presence?**
> ⁸**If I go up to the heavens, you are there;**
> **if I make my bed in the depths, you are there.**
> ⁹**If I rise on the wings of the dawn,**
> **if I settle on the far side of the sea,**
> ¹⁰**even there your hand will guide me,**
> **your right hand will hold me fast.**
> ¹¹**If I say, "Surely the darkness will hide me**
> **and the light become night around me,"**
> ¹²**even the darkness will not be dark to you;**
> **the night will shine like the day,**
> **for darkness is as light to you.**

This section begins with the same ambiguity as the first section. It sounds as if David is trying to escape from God's presence, but as the psalm progresses, it becomes clear that David's talk of escape is hypothetical and that he rejoices in the presence of God.

The "depths" (Hebrew: *Sheol*) in which God is present may refer to hell, since the depths are contrasted with heaven, or the heavens. Although the people in hell do not experience God's gracious presence, even those in hell will recognize that it is the Lord, not Satan, who is the master of hell. There is no place so high or so low, so far east or so far west, so light or so dark that it is outside the presence of God. This is a great comfort, especially to those who are suffering. No persecutor's dungeon is too dark for God to see his people. No prison camp is too filthy for him to be present with them. Wherever they are, he will be with them.

*Almighty*

> ¹³For you created my inmost being;
> you knit me together in my mother's womb.
> ¹⁴I praise you
> because I am fearfully and wonderfully made;
> your works are wonderful,
> I know that full well.
> ¹⁵My frame was not hidden from you
> when I was made in the secret place.
> When I was woven together
> in the depths of the earth,
> ¹⁶your eyes saw my unformed body.
> All the days ordained for me were written
> in your book
> before one of them came to be.
>
> ¹⁷How precious to me are your thoughts,
> O God! How vast is the sum of them!
> ¹⁸Were I to count them,
> they would outnumber the grains of sand.
> When I awake, I am still with you.

This section meditates on one aspect of God's mighty power—his power of creation. Although God does not create us directly from the ground or from a rib, as he did Adam and Eve, the Lord is nonetheless our Creator just as much as he was theirs. Although he brings us into existence through the natural processes of conception and birth, he nevertheless remains fully in control of our creation. He maintains the processes and watches over us with a personal care even before our birth. He shapes us as he shaped Adam, so that it can be said that we were made in "the depths of the earth." Like Adam, we came from the dust and will return to it.

Although these verses do not address the issue of abortion directly, they are certainly relevant to it. The unborn child is being shaped and cared for by God, and God has already ordained his days for him. So a human being who interferes and cuts off the life that God is developing is certainly usurping a right that belongs to the Creator alone. As the giver of life, God alone has the right to take it.

The concluding verses of this section respond to the first three sections of the psalm. God's knowledge, his presence, and his power all cause us to rejoice. God's attributes are not separable qualities that can be considered by themselves. In discussing each attribute of God, we are simply looking at the same loving care for us from a different angle. He uses his power, his presence, his knowledge, and all his other attributes to provide his blessings, which are too numerous to count. "To awake in the presence of God" (verse 18) may well look beyond God's day-to-day preservation of our lives to the resurrection in his presence.

*Holy*
> ¹⁹**If only you would slay the wicked, O God!**
> **Away from me, you bloodthirsty men!**

²⁰**They speak of you with evil intent;**
   **your adversaries misuse your name.**

²¹ **Do I not hate those who hate you, O LORD,**
   **and abhor those who rise up against you?**
²²**I have nothing but hatred for them;**
   **I count them my enemies.**

²³ **Search me, O God, and know my heart;**
   **test me and know my anxious thoughts.**
²⁴**See if there is any offensive way in me,**
   **and lead me in the way everlasting.**

God's attribute of love does not destroy his attribute of holiness. The same God who is the loving forgiver of sins will continue to be the holy punisher of unforgiven sin throughout all eternity. If we love righteousness, we must hate and oppose wickedness. If we love God, we must hate and oppose his enemies. Psalm 5 clearly proclaims God's hatred of sinners. This message is a sharp proclamation of God's law. We must accept even God's strongest judgments against sin as true justice. All of his ways are right.

David closes not with pride but with humility. He recognizes that without forgiveness he too would fall under the wrath of the holy God. David circles back to the beginning of the psalm and asks that the Lord would use his knowledge of David to cleanse him from every evil way that would lead him away from God. For sinners the only solution to God's holy anger against sin is the love of God. This love moves him to use his knowledge and power to save us, rather than to destroy us. This love opens the way of life everlasting.

Israelite mother, child, midwife

# Psalm 140

## *Rescue me from evil men*

Psalm 140 is similar to the many psalms in Books 1 and 2 that deal with the slanderous attacks of David's enemies. Like those psalms, it calls upon the Lord to rescue David and to judge his enemies.

**For the director of music. A psalm of David.**

¹Rescue me, O LORD, from evil men;
  protect me from men of violence,
²who devise evil plans in their hearts
  and stir up war every day.
³They make their tongues as sharp as a serpent's;
  the poison of vipers is on their lips.

*Selah*

⁴Keep me, O LORD, from the hands of the wicked;
  protect me from men of violence
      who plan to trip my feet.
⁵Proud men have hidden a snare for me;
  they have spread out the cords of their net
  and have set traps for me along my path.

*Selah*

⁶O LORD, I say to you, "You are my God."
  Hear, O LORD, my cry for mercy.
⁷O Sovereign LORD, my strong deliverer,
  who shields my head in the day of battle—
⁸do not grant the wicked their desires,
  O LORD; do not let their plans succeed,
  or they will become proud.

*Selah*

⁹Let the heads of those who surround me
  be covered with the trouble their lips have caused.

¹⁰ Let burning coals fall upon them;
may they be thrown into the fire,
into miry pits, never to rise.
¹¹ Let slanderers not be established in the land;
may disaster hunt down men of violence.

¹² I know that the Lᴏʀᴅ secures justice for the poor
and upholds the cause of the needy.
¹³ Surely the righteous will praise your name
and the upright will live before you.

Although the opening section is a prayer for deliverance, its main feature is a description of the treachery of David's enemies. They speak poisonous words and plot evil against the innocent. Their wickedness demonstrates the depths of human depravity.

David realizes that his only hope is in the Lord, so he turns to him. David's call for judgment upon his enemies is motivated by three concerns: that God's promises come true so that God's honor may be upheld, that David be protected, and that the enemies be turned from their arrogant pride.

David's call for judgment on his enemies is expressed in the same spirit as the imprecatory psalms that we have studied previously, including Psalms 137 and 139.

As he usually does, David concludes with an expression of confidence in the Lord's help. The psalm ends with the upright rejoicing in God's presence.

# Psalm 141

### *Guard my lips and heart*

David prays that he will be preserved from the temptations and attacks of the ungodly.

A psalm of David.

[1] O L<small>ORD</small>, I call to you; come quickly to me.
  Hear my voice when I call to you.
[2] May my prayer be set before you like incense;
  may the lifting up of my hands be
        like the evening sacrifice.

[3] Set a guard over my mouth, O L<small>ORD</small>;
  keep watch over the door of my lips.
[4] Let not my heart be drawn to what is evil,
  to take part in wicked deeds with men
        who are evildoers;
  let me not eat of their delicacies.

[5] Let a righteous man strike me—
  it is a kindness;
  let him rebuke me—
  it is oil on my head.
  My head will not refuse it.

  Yet my prayer is ever against the deeds
        of evildoers;
[6] their rulers will be thrown down from the cliffs,
  and the wicked will learn
        that my words were well spoken.
[7] ⌊They will say,⌋ "As one plows
        and breaks up the earth,
  so our bones have been scattered
        at the mouth of the grave."

[8] But my eyes are fixed on you, O Sovereign L<small>ORD</small>;
  in you I take refuge—do not give me over to death.
[9] Keep me from the snares they have laid for me,
  from the traps set by evildoers.
[10] Let the wicked fall into their own nets,
  while I pass by in safety.

In his opening appeal, David compares his prayer to incense and to the sacrifices that were offered to the Lord in the temple. Like those offerings, David's prayers would ascend to the Lord as expressions from a devoted heart. This verse has been a traditional part of our liturgy for evening services.

David prays that he will be kept free from sins of thought, word, and deed. Sins of speech receive special emphasis in the Bible because they are so difficult to avoid and because they so often lead to other sins and to greater strife. Sin often makes its first appearance in words, but it begins invisibly in the heart and mind. David prays that he will not be misled by the schemes and seductive invitations of the ungodly and that he will not covet the luxuries which they obtain immorally. If his heart is safeguarded, he will not join in their evil deeds nor share their ill-gotten gains.

One of the most important ways in which the Lord guards our lives from sin is through the admonition and encouragement we receive from fellow Christians. We should gladly accept well-founded rebukes, for they guard us against becoming entangled in sin. We should also be ready to give such admonition to others in a spirit of love and humility, for in so doing we will help them guard their lives from sin. Today when Christian admonition is often reluctantly given and grudgingly received, we need to cultivate a faithful use of this important aid to Christian life.

The relationship of verse 7 to the rest of the text is difficult to determine with certainty. The NIV understands it as a description of the fate of the wicked and adds the words "They will say" to the text to clarify this interpretation. According to the other interpretation, the verse could be joined with the following verses and understood as a description of the suffering of the righteous at the hands of the wicked.

David is determined to practice and to encourage what is good. He is equally determined to oppose evil and evildoers. Because David does not intend to compromise with evil and insincerity, he rightly expects to experience the hostility that such an uncompromising attitude provokes from the world. But David boldly proclaims God's judgment against the wicked and prays that he will be kept safe from their evil schemes. His hope will remain fastened upon the Lord.

# Psalm 142

## *When my spirit grows faint*

Psalm 142 is a prayer for deliverance from the wicked, which is similar to many of the psalms in the first two books of Psalms. The heading associates this psalm with one of the occasions when David spared Saul in a cave (1 Samuel 22 or 24). Psalm 57 is addressed to the same situation in David's life.

A *maskil* of David. When he was in the cave. A prayer.

¹I cry aloud to the Lᴏʀᴅ;
 I lift up my voice to the Lᴏʀᴅ for mercy.
²I pour out my complaint before him;
 before him I tell my trouble.

³When my spirit grows faint within me,
 it is you who know my way.

 In the path where I walk
 men have hidden a snare for me.
⁴Look to my right and see;
 no one is concerned for me.
 I have no refuge;
 no one cares for my life.

<sup>5</sup>**I cry to you, O LORD;**
**I say, "You are my refuge,**
**my portion in the land of the living."**

<sup>6</sup>**Listen to my cry,**
**for I am in desperate need;**
**rescue me from those who pursue me,**
**for they are too strong for me.**
<sup>7</sup>**Set me free from my prison,**
**that I may praise your name.**

**Then the righteous will gather about me**
**because of your goodness to me.**

Although this psalm was written for a specific trial in David's life, it speaks in such general terms that it would be appropriate for almost any persecution a Christian might suffer.

The psalm begins and ends with appeals to the Lord for help and with expressions of confidence that such help will be provided.

Verse 3 is a beautiful prayer for times of confusion and uncertainty. When we are weary and confused, God knows our way. He understands our problems and knows what will be best for us. This verse reminds us of the more complete description of God's knowledge and presence in Psalm 139.

David is concerned about two groups of people. One group is his enemies, the adherents of Saul, who are determined to destroy him. He sees little prospect for peace and reconciliation with them. A defeat of their plans against him is the only solution. The second group is the indifferent fence-straddlers, who want to sit the conflict out and not get involved.

God's actions on David's behalf will lead the righteous among the uncommitted to recognize David as the king chosen by the Lord. They will then support David's rise to the kingship as a fulfillment of God's will. Saul's son Jonathan was an outstanding example of those who recognized David as the king chosen by God, because of God's blessing upon David. Throughout David's flight from Saul, a growing number of supporters, who eventually formed the nucleus of David's government, joined him in exile. Thus the goodness of the Lord not only saved David from Saul, but also began to build a loyal group of supporters for him.

# Psalm 143

## *Do not bring your servant into judgment*

Psalm 143 is the last of the seven traditional penitential psalms. However, the penitential portion of the psalm forms only a small part of the whole. Most of the psalm is an appeal for relief from the oppression of enemies. In this respect it is similar to many other psalms of David.

**A psalm of David.**

**¹O Lord, hear my prayer,**
**listen to my cry for mercy;**
**in your faithfulness and righteousness**
**come to my relief.**

**²Do not bring your servant into judgment,**
**for no one living is righteous before you.**

David does not base his prayer on his own worthiness before God. Although, relatively speaking, David is the innocent party in the conflicts with Saul and Absalom, he recognizes that his own sins make him unworthy of claiming any blessings from the Lord. He bases his appeal on the

Lord's faithfulness to his promises and upon the righteousness according to which God forgives the sins of all who believe in Christ. David asks to be judged not on the basis of his record but on the basis of his relationship with God. Because David is a child of God through faith, he can call upon the Lord for help.

After establishing his relationship with God as the basis of his prayer, David addresses the rest of the psalm to the oppression he is receiving from his enemies.

> [3] **The enemy pursues me,**
> **he crushes me to the ground;**
> **he makes me dwell in darkness like those long dead.**
>
> [4] **So my spirit grows faint within me;**
> **my heart within me is dismayed.**
> [5] **I remember the days of long ago;**
> **I meditate on all your works**
> **and consider what your hands have done.**
> [6] **I spread out my hands to you;**
> **my soul thirsts for you like a parched land.**
>
> ***Selah***
>
> [7] **Answer me quickly, O LORD;**
> **my spirit fails.**
> **Do not hide your face from me**
> **or I will be like those who go down to the pit.**
> [8] **Let the morning bring me word**
> **of your unfailing love,**
> **for I have put my trust in you.**
> **Show me the way I should go,**
> **for to you I lift up my soul.**
> [9] **Rescue me from enemies, O LORD,**
> **for I hide myself in you.**
> [10] **Teach me to do your will,**
> **for you are my God;**
> **may your good Spirit lead me on level ground.**

<sup>11</sup>**For your name's sake, O Lord,**
  **preserve my life;**
  **in your righteousness,**
  **bring me out of trouble.**
<sup>12</sup>**In your unfailing love,**
  **silence my enemies;**
  **destroy all my foes,**
  **for I am your servant.**

Repeatedly throughout this appeal, David mentions his relationship with God as the basis of his prayer. He also confesses the weakness that assails him at times, but he overcomes this weakness by thinking about the Lord's great deeds in the past. God's past performance and his unfailing love make David confident for the future.

David, however, wants more than deliverance from danger. He also desires the faith and the wisdom to use his victory wisely in a God-pleasing way. For this reason he asks for divine instruction and guidance. He is not interested in the Lord only to be bailed out in a crisis, but he thirsts for a relationship with God that will regulate his whole life.

We too need to beware of thinking of God as a fire extinguisher that we pull out in an emergency and then put back into storage until another crisis arises. We ask for life and health on this earth for a reason: that we may devote ourselves fully to the service of the Lord. We pray, "For your name's sake, O Lord, preserve my life."

# Psalm 144

## *Prayer for the nation*

Psalm 144 is a fitting conclusion to the Davidic collection, since it reflects the period of David's triumph during which he was fully in control of the kingdom. In this respect it parallels Psalm 18. Here David thanks the Lord for victory and prays for further blessing on the nation.

**Of David.**

*A prayer for victory*

<sup>1</sup>Praise be to the LORD my Rock,
  who trains my hands for war,
  my fingers for battle.
<sup>2</sup>He is my loving God and my fortress,
  my stronghold and my deliverer,
  my shield, in whom I take refuge,
  who subdues peoples under me.

<sup>3</sup>O LORD, what is man that you care for him,
  the son of man that you think of him?
<sup>4</sup>Man is like a breath;
  his days are like a fleeting shadow.

<sup>5</sup>Part your heavens, O LORD, and come down;
  touch the mountains, so that they smoke.
<sup>6</sup>Send forth lightning and scatter ⌊the enemies⌋;
  shoot your arrows and rout
          them.
<sup>7</sup>Reach down your hand from on high;
  deliver me and rescue me from the mighty waters,
  from the hands of foreigners
<sup>8</sup>whose mouths are full of lies,
  whose right hands are deceitful.

<sup>9</sup>I will sing a new song to you, O God;
  on the ten-stringed lyre I will make music to you,
<sup>10</sup>to the One who gives victory to kings,
  who delivers his servant David
          from the deadly sword.

> [11] Deliver me and rescue me
> from the hands of foreigners
> whose mouths are full of lies,
> whose right hands are deceitful.

This psalm has a strong military tone, which is offensive to some present-day readers, but as horrible as war is, there is such a thing as a just and necessary war. God himself is often compared to a soldier, and many of the heroes of the Old Testament were military men who fought to protect the good from the evil. David recognized that his military abilities were a gift of God to be used for good, not for evil purposes.

He further recognized that even the best and most capable leaders are short-lived and undependable. A nation's strength must be in the Lord. David therefore calls upon the Lord to descend like a storm on the enemies of his people in order to preserve their freedom to serve him. When God has granted victory and peace, David will lead the people in praising him.

## *The results of victory*

> [12] Then our sons in their youth
> will be like well-nurtured plants,
> and our daughters will be like pillars
> carved to adorn a palace.
> [13] Our barns will be filled
> with every kind of provision.
> Our sheep will increase by thousands,
> by tens of thousands in our fields;
> [14] our oxen will draw heavy loads.
>
> There will be no breaching of walls,
> no going into captivity,
> no cry of distress in our streets.
>
> [15] Blessed are the people of whom this is true;
> blessed are the people whose God is the LORD.

Peace, prosperity, and moral strength are the greatest blessings for a nation. During the period of the judges, Israel rarely had any of these three blessings. The lack of moral strength led to the lack of peace and prosperity. During the reigns of David and Solomon, Israel enjoyed a measure of peace and prosperity that exceeded what had been previously experienced. Although David fell into sin and the downward slide into idolatry began already in Solomon's reign, their reigns were a time of relative moral strength, which contributed to the well-being of the nation.

One of the most important products any society can produce is a generation of children who have not only physical strength and health, but also moral and spiritual strength. Children who have such strength are like well-nurtured plants and steady pillars, since they will be a joy and a blessing to their parents and to the society in which they live. We have reason to fear that our society is increasingly failing to provide such moral strength for its coming generations.

Although our nation is not God's chosen people in the sense that Israel was, we are a nation richly blessed with material prosperity and religious liberty. But already in earthly life, nations tend to reap what they sow. If we stress material things and neglect the moral and spiritual training of the next generation, we can expect to reap a sad harvest of lawlessness, disrespect, and selfishness. If a nation trusts in economic and military might as its salvation, nothing will save it from the judgment of God. God alone is the true source of blessing for any nation.

# Psalm 145

### *The Lord is worthy of praise*

Psalm 145 is a bridge between the last collection of Davidic psalms and the hallelujah psalms that conclude the psalter. Like the preceding psalms, it has a heading ascribing authorship to David. Like the following psalms, it is an outburst of praise to the Lord for his greatness and goodness. The psalm alternates sections of praise, in which David declares his intention to glorify the Lord, and sections of proclamation, in which he describes the greatness of the Lord.

This psalm is an alphabetic acrostic.

**A psalm of praise. Of David.**

*Praise*

**¹I will exalt you, my God the King;
I will praise your name for ever and ever.
²Every day I will praise you
and extol your name for ever and ever.**

*Proclamation of his greatness*

**³Great is the LORD and most worthy of praise;
his greatness no one can fathom.**

*Praise*

**⁴One generation will commend your works to another;
they will tell of your mighty acts.
⁵They will speak of the glorious splendor
of your majesty,
and I will meditate on your wonderful works.
⁶They will tell of the power of your awesome works,
and I will proclaim your great deeds.
⁷They will celebrate your abundant goodness
and joyfully sing of your righteousness.**

*Proclamation of his grace*

**⁸The LORD is gracious and compassionate,
slow to anger and rich in love.**

⁹The LORD is good to all;
he has compassion on all he has made.

## *Praise*

¹⁰All you have made will praise you, O LORD;
your saints will extol you.
¹¹They will tell of the glory of your kingdom
and speak of your might,
¹²so that all men may know of your mighty acts
and the glorious splendor of your kingdom.

## *Proclamation of his kingdom*

¹³Your kingdom is an everlasting kingdom,
and your dominion endures through all generations.
The LORD is faithful to all his promises
and loving toward all he has made.
¹⁴The LORD upholds all those who fall
and lifts up all who are bowed down.
¹⁵The eyes of all look to you,
and you give them their food at the proper time.
¹⁶You open your hand
and satisfy the desires of every living thing.
¹⁷The LORD is righteous in all his ways
and loving toward all he has made.
¹⁸The LORD is near to all who call on him,
to all who call on him in truth.
¹⁹He fulfills the desires of those who fear him;
he hears their cry and saves them.
²⁰The LORD watches over all who love him,
but all the wicked he will destroy.

## *Praise*

²¹My mouth will speak in praise of the LORD.
Let every creature praise his holy name
for ever and ever.

In the sections of praise, David stresses both his personal devotion to praising the Lord and the devotion that the rest of God's people share with him. This fellowship extends across space and time. David has received the message from his ancestors, and he will pass it on to the next generation. This balance between the personal and corporate aspects of worship is emphasized in the second praise section, in which David alternates between the personal "I" and the congregational "they." An important purpose of this chorus of praise is that others who do not yet acknowledge the Lord will learn of his greatness and share in the glory of his kingdom. Finally, the whole universe is summoned to praise the Lord.

The sections that proclaim the Lord's greatness are overwhelmingly positive. There is only one brief mention of his judgment against his enemies. The emphasis is upon the Lord's love, which moves him to provide for his whole creation. Verses 15 and 16 are familiar as a table prayer based on this providential goodness. A second emphasis is the Lord's special love and care for his people. He hears the prayers of his people and delivers the lowly from oppression. He forgives and restores his people when they have sinned. Verse 8 quotes Exodus 34:6, the proclamation of grace that the Lord gave to Moses after the idolatry at Mount Sinai. This verse appears frequently throughout the Old Testament.

This psalm provides an excellent concluding summary for Psalms, since it emphasizes the providential and redemptive love of the Lord, which is the theme of the whole book. It leads us into the final doxology with the invitation "Let every creature praise his holy name."

# Psalms 146–150:
# The Closing Doxology

Psalms 146 to 150 provide a doxology not only to Book 5 but to the whole book of Psalms. Each call to praise has a slightly different emphasis. Taken together they call on all of God's creation to praise him for all his works. Each of these psalms is bracketed by the Hebrew expression "hallelujah," which the NIV has translated "Praise the Lord."

# Psalm 146

### *Praise him for protection*

Psalm 146 is similar to Psalm 145, which also speaks of the Lord's protection and provision for his people. It contrasts the help of earthly rulers, who are short-lived and undependable, with the help of the Lord, who is trustworthy and eternal.

¹ **Praise the LORD.**

**Praise the LORD, O my soul.**
² **I will praise the LORD all my life;**
  **I will sing praise to my God as long as I live.**

³ **Do not put your trust in princes,**
  **in mortal men, who cannot save.**
⁴ **When their spirit departs,**
  **they return to the ground;**
  **on that very day their plans come to nothing.**

⁵ **Blessed is he whose help is the God of Jacob,**
  **whose hope is in the LORD his God,**

⁶the Maker of heaven and earth,
 the sea, and everything in them—
 the LORD, who remains faithful forever.
⁷He upholds the cause of the oppressed
 and gives food to the hungry.
 The LORD sets prisoners free,
⁸the LORD gives sight to the blind,
 the LORD lifts up those who are bowed down,
 the LORD loves the righteous.
⁹The LORD watches over the alien
 and sustains the fatherless and the widow,
 but he frustrates the ways of the wicked.

¹⁰ The LORD reigns forever,
 your God, O Zion, for all generations.

Praise the LORD.

The opening line is an invitation in the plural, intended for all people. The next three lines are the personal response of the psalmist to this invitation. His whole life will be devoted to praise.

The influential and powerful of the world, even the best of them, cannot be our ultimate source of confidence. Like Adam, all of them are dust and will return to the ground from which they came.

The book of Psalms begins with the word "blessed." Verse 5 of Psalm 146 begins the last blessing in this book of blessings. Although there is brief mention of the food the Lord provides for his people, the main focus of the psalm is on the protecting power of the Lord, which raises the lowly, frees the prisoners, and gives sight to the blind.

We think of the dramatic way the Lord did this through the ministry of Jesus. His ministry reminds us that the greatest gifts are not natural food, physical healing, and political freedom, but spiritual food, which gives eternal life; healing that frees us from sin and death; and freedom that will endure forever. These blessings the Lord provided for his people through the messianic King, whom he sent to them. For these blessings we praise the Lord now and forever.

# Psalm 147

## *Praise him for providing*

Although Psalm 147 contains several references to God's protection of his people, the main emphasis has shifted from that of Psalm 146. The emphasis now lies on the creative power by which the Lord sustains the universe. This psalm has ties with the concluding chapters of Job, with Isaiah chapter 40, and with such psalms as Psalm 104.

Verses 2 and 3, 12 and 13 would have been especially meaningful in the time of Nehemiah.

<sup>1</sup> **Praise the LORD.**

**How good it is to sing praises to our God,
how pleasant and fitting to praise him!**

<sup>2</sup> **The LORD builds up Jerusalem;
he gathers the exiles of Israel.**
<sup>3</sup> **He heals the brokenhearted
and binds up their wounds.**

<sup>4</sup> **He determines the number of the stars
and calls them each by name.**
<sup>5</sup> **Great is our LORD and mighty in power;
his understanding has no limit.**

⁶ The LORD sustains the humble
  but casts the wicked to the ground.
⁷ Sing to the LORD with thanksgiving;
  make music to our God on the harp.

⁸ He covers the sky with clouds;
  he supplies the earth with rain
  and makes grass grow on the hills.
⁹ He provides food for the cattle
  and for the young ravens when they call.

¹⁰ His pleasure is not in the strength of the horse,
  nor his delight in the legs of a man;
¹¹ the LORD delights in those who fear him,
  who put their hope in his unfailing love.

¹² Extol the LORD, O Jerusalem;
  praise your God, O Zion,
¹³ for he strengthens the bars of your gates
  and blesses your people within you.
¹⁴ He grants peace to your borders
  and satisfies you with the finest of wheat.

¹⁵ He sends his command to the earth;
  his word runs swiftly.
¹⁶ He spreads the snow like wool
  and scatters the frost like ashes.
¹⁷ He hurls down his hail like pebbles.
  Who can withstand his icy blast?
¹⁸ He sends his word and melts them;
  he stirs up his breezes,
  and the waters flow.

¹⁹ He has revealed his word to Jacob,
  his laws and decrees to Israel.

**²⁰ He has done this for no other nation;
they do not know his laws.**

**Praise the LORD.**

The greatness of God's power is shown by his knowledge and control of the stars, but his power that is most practical for us lies closer at hand. An outstanding example is his management of the waters of the earth. Through the water cycle of evaporation and precipitation, through clouds and rain, snow and hail, streams and oceans, he provides water for the earth so that all his creatures will receive their food.

If he withdraws his sustaining power and blessing from this process, the result will be drought, loss, hunger, and finally even starvation. As this commentary was being written, the United States was experiencing one of the most severe droughts in memory. Such events, whenever they occur, remind us not to presume on the Lord's goodness nor to take his blessings for granted.

God's Word by which he commands nature and his Word by which he communicates with human beings are set side by side in the last portions of the psalm. Although nature gives abundant testimony to the Lord's goodness, we need the revelation of his Word to reach a full and clear understanding of God's goodness in providing for us. We need such revelation for a clear knowledge of who our Creator and provider is. Israel had such knowledge. We do too.

Such knowledge enables us to see the hand of God in nature more clearly. Such knowledge should lead us to receive his blessings with thanksgiving and to use them in ways that are pleasing to him. God's greatest delight in creation is not the strength and marvelous abilities with which he has endowed his creatures, but the humble faith and loving trust that his children return to him. It is good, pleasant, and fitting to praise him for his marvelous works.

Israelites gathering wheat

# Psalm 148

## *Praise him, all creation*

All creation, visible and invisible, animate and inanimate, is called to praise the Lord. Psalm 148 starts with the angels, sweeps through the created universe, and ends with God's people. Together they form a vast choir, which sings his praises.

The psalm is arranged chiastically, moving from the rational to the inanimate creatures in the heavens and then in reverse order, from the inanimate to the rational on earth.

> [1] **Praise the LORD.**

### *Praise from the heavens*

> **Praise the LORD from the heavens,**
> **praise him in the heights above.**
> [2] **Praise him, all his angels,**
> **praise him, all his heavenly hosts.**
>
> [3] **Praise him, sun and moon,**
> **praise him, all you shining stars.**
> [4] **Praise him, you highest heavens**
> **and you waters above the skies.**
>
> [5] **Let them praise the name of the LORD,**
> **for he commanded and they were created.**
> [6] **He set them in place for ever and ever;**
> **he gave a decree that will never pass away.**

The angels and the heavenly bodies are often placed side by side in the Scriptures, especially in poetic parallelism. The term "heavenly hosts" (verse 2) may refer to either of them. The heathen often worshiped spirits and the heavenly bodies.

Though they are the most majestic and awesome of God's creatures, they are nevertheless creations whom the psalmist summons to praise their Creator.

## *Praise from the earth*

⁷Praise the LORD from the earth,
  you great sea creatures and all ocean depths,
⁸lightning and hail, snow and clouds,
  stormy winds that do his bidding,
⁹you mountains and all hills,
  fruit trees and all cedars,
¹⁰wild animals and all cattle,
  small creatures and flying birds,
¹¹kings of the earth and all nations,
  you princes and all rulers on earth,
¹²young men and maidens,
  old men and children.

¹³ Let them praise the name of the LORD,
  for his name alone is exalted;
  his splendor is above the earth and the heavens.
¹⁴He has raised up for his people a horn,
  the praise of all his saints,
  of Israel, the people close to his heart.

  Praise the LORD.

The praise that nature renders to the Lord is also prominent in Psalms 96 to 98. Refer to the commentary on those psalms for a discussion of the manner in which the creation participates both in the effects of the fall and in redemption. The created world will share in the freedom and joy of our redemption.

Verses 13 and 14 are a transition to Psalm 149, which emphasizes the praise of God's people. The horn God raises up for his people is the ruler he provides for them. In a lesser sense, this term can refer to a king of Israel. In the full sense, it refers to the King of kings, Jesus the Messiah.

It is fitting that this invitation to praise, which is addressed to all creation, should direct our attention to the One who has been given all power in heaven and on earth. It is fitting that as the book of Psalms draws to an end, our praise is directed to the Messiah. His rule has been the theme around which the book of Psalms revolves. He is the praise of God's people.

# Psalm 149

### *Praise him, all his people*

Like the preceding psalm, Psalm 149 has thematic ties with Psalms 96 to 98, especially with Psalm 98, which speaks both of the joy God finds in his people and of his coming for judgment.

> [1] **Praise the LORD.**
>
> **Sing to the LORD a new song,**
> **his praise in the assembly of the saints.**
> [2] **Let Israel rejoice in their Maker;**
> **let the people of Zion be glad in their King.**
> [3] **Let them praise his name with dancing**
> **and make music to him with tambourine and harp.**
> [4] **For the LORD takes delight in his people;**
> **he crowns the humble with salvation.**
> [5] **Let the saints rejoice in this honor**
> **and sing for joy on their beds.**
>
> [6] **May the praise of God be in their mouths**
> **and a double-edged sword in their hands,**

<sup>7</sup>to inflict vengeance on the nations
  and punishment on the peoples,
<sup>8</sup>to bind their kings with fetters,
  their nobles with shackles of iron,
<sup>9</sup>to carry out the sentence written against them.
  This is the glory of all his saints.

**Praise the LORD.**

The first section describes the exuberant, joyful praise that Israel poured out during its festivals. There is no evidence that dance and the tambourine were used in the temple worship itself, but they were a normal part of festive processions, such as that in which David brought the ark of the covenant to Jerusalem. The praise described in the last verse of this section is more personal, since it takes place in the privacy of one's own bedroom. Whether together or alone, God's people rejoice in the honor of being members of God's family through the saving work of Christ.

After the joyful outburst in the first half of the psalm, the solemn warning of judgment in the second half of the psalm strikes a jarring note. We should remember that God's deeds of judgment are not the opposite of his compassion for his people, but a part of it. He judges the world to benefit them and to repay the wrongs they have suffered.

Believers join God in the acts of judgment day. The double-edged sword with which they strike God's enemies is the sword of the Word (Revelation 1:16; 19:15; Hebrews 4:12). The law of God, which they have preached, will condemn the world, which ignored it. The gospel the world rejected will increase the world's guilt before God.

The specific way believers will work with Christ on judgment day is not clearly spelled out in Scripture, but it is clearly indicated by such passages as 1 Corinthians 6:2,3, which includes even the evil angels among those whom we shall judge. To be given the glorious privilege of joining Christ in the work of judgment is cause to praise the Lord.

# Psalm 150

### *Praise the Lord!*

This final hallelujah provides a powerful conclusion to this collection of hallelujah psalms and to the whole book of Psalms. In its brief scope it tells us where the Lord should be praised, why he should be praised, how he should be praised, and who should praise him.

> **¹ Praise the LORD.**
>
> **Praise God in his sanctuary;**
> **praise him in his mighty heavens.**
>
> **² Praise him for his acts of power;**
> **praise him for his surpassing greatness.**
>
> **³ Praise him with the sounding of the trumpet,**
> **praise him with the harp and lyre,**
> **⁴ praise him with tambourine and dancing,**
> **praise him with the strings and flute,**
> **⁵ praise him with the clash of cymbals,**
> **praise him with resounding cymbals.**
>
> **⁶ Let everything that has breath praise the LORD.**
> **Praise the LORD.**

The Lord should be praised everywhere. "His sanctuary" (verse 1) may at times refer to heaven, but here it probably refers to his temple on earth, so that the two parts of this verse match the two parts of Psalm 148: praise him on earth and praise him in heaven.

The Lord should be praised for all his works of creation and redemption, which have been described in the preceding psalms.

The Lord should be praised joyfully. Israel's music was joyful and exciting. It used a full range of musical instruments, and on festive occasions dance was a part of religious celebration. Nothing in Scripture suggests that religious music and worship should be limited to the somber or that certain instruments are inherently inappropriate for worship. God should be praised joyfully with everything we have.

Everyone should praise the Lord. All are invited to do so. Through Christ, God has made it possible for all to do so. The psalms have given us ample reason. It is a joy to do so. Let us praise the Lord.

The book of Psalms is a miniature Bible, a miniature history of God's people. It expresses all the feelings and experiences they will ever have. It is fitting that this book ends where our history and our experience will end—in the sanctuary of our God, singing joyful hallelujahs forever. For this we gladly shout, "Praise the Lord!"